# Interviewing Groups and Individuals in Qualitative Market Research

2
QMR

Joanna Chrzanowska

**SAGE Publications**
London • Thousand Oaks • New Delhi

SAGE Publications Ltd
6 Bonhill Street
London EC2A 4PU

SAGE Publications Inc.
2455 Teller Road
Thousand Oaks, California 91320

SAGE Publications India Pvt Ltd
32, M-Block Market
Greater Kailash - I
New Delhi 110 048

**British Library Cataloguing in Publication data**

A catalogue record for this book is available
from the British Library

ISBN 0 7619 7272 2

**Library of Congress Control Number 2002101993**

Typeset by SIVA Math Setters, Chennai, India
Printed in Great Britain by Antony Rowe, Chippenham, Wiltshire

# Contents

# Acknowledgements

Thanks to all the editors for their advice and flexible deadlines – and particularly Gill Ereaut and Mike Imms for their inspiration and encouragement.

A number of people have contributed specifically to this volume, and I thank them all:

Andrea Williams and Wendy Mitchell, RDSi;
Ashley Burleson and Angela Sanchez, The Link Group;
Dr Roger Kneebone;
Elizabeth Vititoe, CSM Inc.;
Fiona Jack, Green Light Research;
Fiona Kennedy, Kennedy Research;
Gillian Rolls-Wilson;
Harry Vardis, Creative Focus Inc.;
Ian Sippitt, Leapfrog Research;
John Rose, The Qualitative Consultancy;
Mark Michelson, Mark Michelson Associates;
Millward Brown;
Nedra Du Broff, Nedra Du Broff Research;
Plaza Research;
Rina Valeny, Context Research;
Angus Jenkinson, Stepping Stones;
Nick Long, NFO MBL;
Alison Leith, TRBI;
Kate Hamilton, Ignite;

Over the years, I have helped to train hundreds of qualitative researchers – and not a few clients. On every course, I have learnt something from them too, and I applaud their enthusiasm, insights and willingness to be open to new ideas.

Finally, the author and publishers wish to thank the following for permission to reproduce illustrations in this book:

Figure 3.1 © World Advertising Center, reproduced from Lannon and Cooper (1983) 'Humanistic advertising: a holistic cultural perspective', *International Journal of Advertising*, 2 (3): 195–213.

Figure 8.4 and 9.1 reproduced from Branthwaite (1995) 'Standardization through creative expression', *Canadian Journal of Research*, 14: 87–93.

# Editorial Introduction

## About Qualitative Market Research: A Background to the Series

*Gill Ereaut, Mike Imms and Martin Callingham*

This series of books explains the theory and practice of qualitative market research, or commercial qualitative research. There is no single agreed definition of qualitative market research but we can paraphrase some key definitions and describe it thus:

> A form of market research that seeks to explore and understand people's attitudes, motivations and behaviours – the 'why' and 'how' behind the 'what' – using methods that seek to reach understanding through dialogue and evocation (rather than measurement). Qualitative research generally attempts to make sense of and interpret phenomena in terms of the meanings people bring to them.

In UK practice, which forms the focus of this series, the most common form of qualitative market research employs the group discussion (or 'focus group') and depth interview as its major field methods, although many other methods can be and are increasingly used, such as observational approaches.

Common to all methods is the aim of getting beyond public, conscious factors – those things that people can and will say in response to simple questions. Qualitative market research provides effective ways of exploring such issues as private thoughts and feelings, pre-conscious factors (such as intuitive associations, the taken-for-granted, habitual and culturally derived attitudes and behaviours), and the important issue of emotions. Also used within qualitative market research are techniques that enable researchers to overcome the limitations of the verbal.

The main objectives of qualitative market research usually involve one or more of the following:

- **Diagnosis** – providing depth of understanding of a current situation, of why things are the way they are.
- **Prognosis** – providing guidance on likely responses to options, plans or proposals.

- **Creativity** – using respondents in qualitative market research as a source of ideas, innovation and inspiration.

What users of qualitative market research have in common is a need for *understanding and sense-making*.

- It aims to reveal deep and specific understanding of activities, choices and attitudes relevant to client concerns across a range of stakeholders. These stakeholders are not simply consumers and customers, users of the goods and services of commercial organisations – increasingly qualitative market research is used by a wide range of not-for-profit organisations.
- The insights generated include an understanding of the interrelationships of issues, as well as the detail of individual issues.
- Qualitative market research offers a conceptual and not just descriptive view of these issues.
- It may also serve to codify tacit and informal knowledge of the external world and make it accessible to organisations.

It is hard to pinpoint the exact date and place of birth of commercial qualitative research but essentially it is a phenomenon of the post-Second World War era and arose in response to changing information needs of organisations. Initially it was marketers who began to recognise that meeting consumer wants and needs required a level of understanding of people's motivations, usage and attitudes that went beyond measurement of the 'simple, hard facts' accessible to survey methods.

The qualitative market research profession has undoubtedly 'come of age' – with an established and respected role within the decision-making procedures of a wide and diverse variety of commercial, not-for-profit and public sector organisations across the globe. It is hard to find any *commercial* organisation that does *not* now use qualitative market research, but within the past decade or so the range of organisations using commercial qualitative market research to aid organisational decision-making has broadened considerably. Qualitative market research has become a valuable tool for anyone who needs to take account of any 'stakeholder' groups – not just consumers and customers but also staff, users of public services, supporters, voters, inmates and so on.

The evolution of the qualitative market research profession has several distinctive characteristics.

- It has apparently evolved in parallel with, but completely separately from, the academic qualitative research community which exists today across many disciplines in the social sciences and humanities.
- Relatively few textbooks have been written about qualitative market research and many external commentators have noted that the

profession has a sparse literature, and limited discussion of issues that concern academic researchers, such as epistemology.

- The early qualitative market researchers drew on a body of theory that came principally from psychology, but over the decades this has broadened to include other social sciences disciplines and methods (anthropology, sociology, cultural analysis, semiotics etc.), as well as continuing to develop methodology from emergent trends in psychology.
- Theory has tended to be incorporated and used in qualitative market research in a 'serendipitous' way. Few qualitative market researchers have been interested in theory for its own sake, but only for its utility value, applicability and usefulness in meeting clients' needs for relevant information and insights. A key characteristic of commercial qualitative market research is its eclecticism and important benefits arise from this *absence* of theoretical or methodological purism.

Why has this series been created? First, the industry has an essentially 'oral' tradition and a major aim of this series has been to record this tradition in written form. Simply setting down what is common practice, along with beliefs about why things are done like this, has not been done before in such a comprehensive way. Like all oral traditions, that of the qualitative research industry sometimes lacks consistency and its 'narrators' do not always agree on its origins. We make no apology for the fact that the reader will find evidence of this in slightly differing accounts and differing attributions of key principles. One of the benefits of creating this series is that such differences become manifest and can be debated and perhaps reconciled by future writers on commercial qualitative market research.

Secondly, as the industry has grown in size and matured, and as its body of (largely tacit) knowledge has grown and broadened, the link between the theories originally informing it and day-to-day practice has tended to weaken. The limited interest in questions of methodology and theory for their own sake warrants comment – and there are probably two main reasons for this.

- First, the nature of clients' demand for commercial qualitative market research means that its value rests solely on the value of the *findings themselves* – rather than the detailed means of reaching those findings.
- Secondly, client organisations have, for the same reason, consistently shown little interest in theory – it has restricted commercial value in commercial qualitative market research.

This is in contrast to much academic qualitative research, where the contributions of a study to methodological and theoretical knowledge may be regarded as at least as valuable as the substantive findings themselves, and certainly need to be reported. There is now more interest within qualitative market research in understanding the roots of everyday practice in order to enhance training and professional development.

Thus a second key aim of this series is to attempt to re-connect practice to theory.

Commercial qualitative market research has until very recently focused almost, though not entirely, on interview-based methods – 'groups and depths'. This is quite different from much academic qualitative research, which draws on a far broader range of methods. Here again, the reasons have to do with the nature of the demand for commercial qualitative market research. In short, the commercial qualitative market research industry has very effectively 'systematised' interview-based qualitative procedures. In consequence there is a large and established market *and* a commercially viable established 'going rate' for interview-based commercial qualitative research that simply does not exist, at least at present, for other methods.

Within the limitations of interviewing methods, commercial qualitative market research has been incredibly creative. This creativity ranges from the application of sophisticated projective and enabling techniques and extensive use of stimulus material, to differing moderating styles, interview lengths, structures and procedures to extend the boundaries of what can be explored and captured within 'groups and depths'.

The qualitative market research business has developed specialisms, involving specific theories, methods and ideas of best practice:

- relating to particular types of respondents – children, business-to-business, staff etc.
- relating to particular types of topic – social policy, advertising development, new product development, packaging design, design and layout of stores, branch offices and websites etc.
- relating to specific business sectors – for example the pharmaceutical industry makes extensive use of qualitative market research, but tends to use quite tailored interview procedures and sampling methods, and specialist moderators.

Representing the full range of practice across all these fields is beyond the scope of this series, which aims to cover the primary research processes within mainstream practice, and two of the major applications of qualitative market research – the development of brands and the development of advertising. To the extent that many general principles, and certain aspects of practice, are shared across many varieties of qualitative market research, it will nevertheless be of relevance to many of these specialists.

The series has been written for the benefit of four main types of reader.

- First, **practitioners** (including those new to the profession) constitute a major audience for the series. By spelling out the key theories and principles that underpin good practice we hope practitioners can use this knowledge to train future generations of qualitative researchers – and also to make more informed choices of methodology and practice. By tracing back relevant theory and linking it to current practice, we aim to raise the conscious competence of current and future practitioners.

- Secondly we hope **users** of qualitative market research will find the series interesting and that it will enable them to make more informed assessments about the kind of contribution qualitative market research can make to organisational decision-making. It should also help them assess the quality of qualitative market research provided by their agencies and to recognise *good* qualitative market research.
- Thirdly, **students** of business and related disciplines may find it a helpful aid to understanding the role and value of qualitative market research in decision-making and how it works in real life practice.
- Finally, **academic qualitative researchers** may find the insight into commercial qualitative market research informative, given that so little is published about it. Commercial confidentiality means that the findings of few commercial qualitative market research projects will ever be made available, but this series at least exposes the principles and practice of qualitative market research in general terms.

In a more general sense, we hope that by being more explicit about what we do and why we do it, we can encourage constructive criticism. Specifically we hope to stimulate debate and to challenge others to identify better and different methods and practices.

All the books in this series have been written by respected qualitative market research practitioners, and as editors we are pleased that an unexpected benefit has arisen. The act of creating this series often involved analysing and setting down current practice for the first time. In so doing, a level of understanding of our business has emerged which was not evident to any of us before undertaking this comprehensive task. This emergent theory is described within several of the books in the series.

## THE SCOPE OF THIS SERIES

The series comprises seven books, covering three broad categories. All the books are written primarily from a UK perspective, but where appropriate, authors have drawn comparisons with other markets, especially the USA.

- Book 1 provides an **introduction to qualitative market research** which contextualises the rest of the series. It also explores why it is that organisations might need qualitative market research and how it fits with their information needs and decision-making processes. This book, in addition, explores important issues not specifically addressed in other volumes, including the detail of project design, and the ethics and professional codes which underpin practice.
- Four other volumes describe the theory and methods of the key **processes** of commercial qualitative market research: interview-based fieldwork (Book 2); other forms of data collection (Book 3); analysis

and interpretation of findings (Book 4); and the development and 'delivery' of recommendations to clients (Book 7).

- Two further volumes – Books 5 and 6 – describe the theory and methods of two of the most significant **applications** of commercial qualitative market research – brand and advertising development.

Before going on to outline the scope and role of this particular book in the series, we would like to acknowledge the many people who helped in different ways to make this series a reality. We would particularly like to thank David Silverman for introducing us to Sage and for encouragement at the early stages; and the team at Sage, especially Michael Carmichael and Vanessa Harwood, for their support.

# About this Book

We have already indicated that interviewing is the cornerstone of qualitative market research field practice, for reasons that are explored in Book 1. It is true that these interviewing methods – largely focus groups and unstructured individual interviews – are increasingly complemented or developed by alternative methods and these are covered in Book 3 in the series, *Methods Beyond Interviewing*. However, the focus group and the individual interview remain the major methods of qualitative market research. In this respect this present volume, which looks at principle and practice in interviewing, represents a key foundational text in the series.

Qualitative market researchers spend a great deal of time interviewing and acquire huge amounts of practical skill and experience. This is true craft skill – group moderation especially, like many skilled crafts, *looks* very easy to do. In a well-run group the discussion will seem to just flow, and the event will look like an informal conversation. The fact that the moderator is working very hard to keep the group on topic, on time and ethically valid is simply not visible. Anyone who has tried to run a group discussion to address a set of topics or objectives will know that it is far from easy.

Book 1 emphasises the tacit nature of much of the qualitative market researcher's knowledge. In interviewing skills in particular, training within the business is overwhelmingly carried out by apprenticeship, and practitioner skills are honed by extensive practice. Experienced researchers may thus find it difficult to articulate exactly what they do and why. Where there is explicit methodological knowledge, this exists largely in the form of an oral tradition, passed down from older to younger researchers. Within the oral tradition there are some taken-for-granted ideas of 'best practice', especially regarding how to structure a group and some broad principles of questioning. This present book explains how some of these ideas are traceable to humanistic psychology and the study of group dynamics, but notes that they are often now disconnected from this theory. The book goes on to explore the way qualitative market research continues its pragmatic and eclectic relationship with theory, in relation to various schools of psychological and other thinking, and to research into brain function and memory.

Listening and eliciting skills are, once learnt, largely taken for granted by experienced practitioners. They, along with strategies for enhancing these processes, are made explicit here and this is likely to be of use and interest to those engaged in qualitative research practice of any kind. This book also illuminates aspects of interviewing practice which are more specific to the practice of qualitative market research – that is, research carried out to specific objectives and under specific conditions. These include specialised knowledge of interviewing in *groups*, and practices that emerge from working to tight objectives and time constraints.

Regarding group moderation in particular, there is within the industry a huge store of tacit knowledge, representing a relatively untapped resource for novices and outsiders alike. This book sets down a great deal of this tacit knowledge – what experienced moderators do to optimise their groups and interviews – and makes it accessible to all. There has until now been little explicit or published knowledge about this kind of detail.

As already noted, group discussions and individual interviews have been the primary methods used to address a very wide range of research questions within market research. Researchers have thus been very inventive in making use of these basic vehicles, often *actively* eliciting information from respondents by the use of various forms of respondent task and material (in doing so moving far from the 'naturalistic' approach of some academic qualitative approaches). Other research materials in various formats are also likely to be used in order to communicate specific ideas to respondents so that they may be explored. This book looks at the issues involved in designing and handling these tasks and materials in order to get the best from the research.

The fieldwork component of a project in market research is not only crucial in terms of collecting good data – it is also one of its most public and visible parts. The way aspects of the process are handled by the researcher are vital to good communication and levels of trust between client and researcher. Competence in interviewing is a basic requirement in qualitative market research, and excellence a significant advantage. This book will allow practical experience, which remains vital to developing this craft skill, to be underpinned and immensely enhanced by an insightful, detailed and assured examination of the principles that lie behind best practice.

# Introduction: The Inside Story of a Focus Group

Interviewing in qualitative market research is a delicate balancing act. There are client and interviewer agendas to integrate, power relations between interviewers and respondents to manage, many options for framing questions and choosing interventions, and a need for sensitivity to group dynamics as well as the feelings and issues of individual respondents.

This book describes how all these processes are managed, but the true integration of processes happens as a set of moment-by-moment interviewer choices. Colloquially speaking, these happen in the interviewer's head; since the interviewer or moderator is working simultaneously on several different levels it might be more accurate to say they happen in the 'bodymind' (using inputs from the physical, emotional and intuitive levels). It is difficult to explain the integration of interviewing processes without an insight into this internal landscape. Therefore this introductory chapter offers a fictionalised account of a focus group from the interviewer's internal perspective. It is based on nearly 30 years' experience of running groups like this, and all of the issues raised by this account are discussed later in the book.

(NB: In this book an interviewer is referred to as a moderator when he or she is working with a group.)

## THE INSIDE STORY

The moderator walked into the room where the group was already waiting. On a coffee table in front of the armchairs was a collection of teenage skin-care products, while four 14-year-old girls studiously avoided the moderator's gaze. Two were chatting animatedly to each other, one was managing to look nowhere in particular, while the fourth was busy applying mascara, despite already wearing far more make-up than the rest. The moderator's heart momentarily sank at the thought of the task ahead – two hours with a group who were already giving the impression they would rather be somewhere else, talking about something else. She quickly reminded herself they were nervous and shy rather than deliberately obstructive – teenagers were especially sensitive to the feeling that they would be judged in a group of this sort. Building the relationships between the girls in the group would be a challenge – and she would have to work out what they imagined her role to be. But she remembered how enjoyable the last group had turned out to be, so with a smile she said, 'Hi everyone! Thanks for coming. We are ready to start now, and I just want to say a few words about what we are doing today. We are gathered here together – oh, whoops, sorry, it's not a wedding ...'

The bad joke at least got her eye contact with the group. She seized the moment to explain that her job was to understand what people thought and felt about the products and the services they used. She herself didn't have any specialist knowledge about these products, which is why she wanted to work with the group to understand whether the products were meeting their needs, and also to ask their feelings about a couple of new ideas. She went on to explain how people had individual preferences so she would not be surprised if the whole group did not agree, and to reassure them it was OK to say if they didn't like something. Another few minutes covered the other necessary information in the introduction (there were some giggles from the girls as they realised they would be taped), and then it was time to find out something about her respondents. Two were clearly friends, while the other two didn't know each other. To even things out she decided to split up the friendship pair and gave the two new pairs the task of finding out some basic things about each other and introducing each other to the rest of the group. The energy level in the group immediately went up as they chatted with each other. Then, with a little embarrassment, and some prompting, they proceeded to describe their new partner's schooling and interests. As various topics were mentioned the moderator checked the experiences of the rest of the group, and after another ten minutes the group had established they had similar tastes in music, read similar magazines, were equally disparaging about the facilities provided for teenagers in their area – but were actually quite different personalities. The quiet girl turned out to be one of the more confident respondents and tended to speak up first, so once or twice the moderator turned to one of the others first to ask a question. A pattern of response established at this stage could carry on throughout the group. The girls had visibly relaxed, so it was time to move on to the real work of the research. The moderator briefly summarised what she had learnt from them so far, carefully noting the differences as well as the similarities between them. Too much emphasis on similarities might send a signal that she was mainly interested in areas of convergence, whereas she wanted them to feel they could disagree at any time.

Then she asked one of the important questions from the brief. The client needed to know how girls made their first choices in skincare, and what repertoire of products and brands they trusted. 'So, thinking now about the various products you buy and use for your face, what do you think influences you?' Silence. More silence. The group had suddenly returned to the avoidant starting position. 'Oh dear,' the moderator said, 'I have a feeling that wasn't a very good question. You do all use things like cleansers for your face, don't you?'

'Yes we do, but we don't buy 'em. We get our mums to get 'em.'

'Oh, I see. Do you all?' (They nodded.) 'Can you tell me a bit more about that?'

'Well, they are expensive, so you try to nag your mum when she goes out shopping – oh, mum, pleeease, can you get me some face wash?'

The moderator looked slightly confused: 'You said they are expensive, but this pack here is less than £2. Are you saying they would be expensive for someone of your age?'

'They are expensive because you don't want to spend your money on 'em,' came the reply. 'You want to get the stuff like lipstick and eyeshadow.'

'Uh huh,' the moderator was intrigued. 'What is it about lipstick and eyeshadow that makes them worth the money?'

'They are more fun –' started one girl, while another pointed out that they made a visible difference to a face. Face wash might be regarded as a necessity, but it didn't do anything visible, except perhaps keep spots away.

The moderator made a mental note to come back to this topic. She was wondering whether this need to have visible changes was perhaps somehow related to experimenting with different identities as a teenager – but now was not the time to ask about this subject. She had not built up the required level of trust with them. Later she would remind the group that they had talked about 'fun' in this context and she would try to understand more about this.

'How do you choose what to ask your mums to get?' She came back to the original question, this time remembering to avoid the phrase 'what influences you?' It was on the client's topic guide, and she really should have spent some time before the group re-phrasing things like that. Many consumers did not like the implication that they were influenced to buy. Unfortunately, the research materials had been delayed en route so she had spent too much time chasing them up instead of reading and integrating the topic guide. She asked each girl by name, establishing eye contact, waiting patiently for them to express themselves, adding supplementary questions to be clear. Then she picked up on some of the general issues that had emerged.

'You said "people" always say you should cleanse before you go to bed and you shouldn't use soap. Who do you mean by "people" exactly?'

'People' evidently included magazine writers, mothers and older sisters, and their close friends. During the course of this elaboration, the moderator was surprised to discover that sleepovers were popular amongst this age group. The genuine surprise came over in her voice: 'Oh, I didn't realise people did that here. I always thought of it as a sort of American thing.' The girls looked at her pityingly and proceeded to describe in detail what happened at a sleepover, and how part of the ritual was to experiment with hairstyles and cosmetics and to try out each other's skin-care products.

This had not been included on the topic guide, but it was a worthwhile bit of exploration. It would be interesting to be a fly on the wall at one of these sleepovers … Thinking about the topic guide reminded her to check progress so far, although she was sure she already had a couple of interesting insights for the client.

She glanced at it now and thought it might be a good idea to establish what they were actually using. The issues related to choosing or buying a product might become clearer if they were actually looking at a product they used. It would make it more real.

'I tell you what,' she said quickly, 'let's just look through all the products on this table, and pick out which ones you are using right now. Feel free to pick them up.'

The energetic rush forward took her slightly by surprise, although it was often the case in groups that handling products raised energy and interest levels. She got the feeling that these products were more interesting than the group had initially suggested. She left the group alone for a good two or three minutes, which felt like a long time, but they were engrossed in examining the products.

'Miss, what are the seven signs of ageing?' The question came out of nowhere, prompted by a description on one of the products they were looking at. From the language used it was evident they were still seeing her as some sort of teacher figure – an idea that must be dispelled if she wanted authentic responses, not teacher-pleasing ones. 'No need to call me miss,' she said, 'you probably know more than I do about most of this stuff.' The thought flashed through the moderator's mind that there was perhaps a gentle challenge implied in that question – perhaps they were making the point that they were indeed very much younger and with unlined skin, while the moderator was at least a generation older. Why else ask that question at that time? She decided to risk a little bit of self-disclosure in order to reassure them that she was not going to pretend to be a teenager in order to gain their trust.

'Well you can probably see at least five of the seven signs of ageing on my face,' she joked, 'but I don't actually use that product so I don't really know what they are.'

The answer seemed satisfactory, and they went back to examining the products, opening pots, looking at the textures of the creams and lotions, sniffing the fragrances. Another quick mental note that obviously in this market there was a need for physical contact with the product – she would ask the client later about the possibilities for samples and testers.

It was becoming increasingly evident that they had disregarded her instruction to pick out the ones they used, since they seemed to be opening the more sophisticated products that were aimed at the older age group she would be interviewing next.

'Are these the ones you actually use?' she checked. Slightly guilty, they explained that these were ones they would like to use, because they had seen them advertised, but they didn't know what they actually did. 'What's an exfoliator?' she was asked. The moderator found herself in a dilemma about answering this question. If she did not answer, she might position herself as a skincare expert and she did not want to be seen as an authority. There again, as an older woman could she credibly pretend not to know? She would try the standard response first; 'What does it sound as if it does?' Blank faces and 'dunno's' convinced her they needed an explanation, but not before the clever one commented 'It sounds as if it takes the leaves off trees!'

The moderator decided to try to leave the authority with the client, so she said, 'Well the people I am doing this research for told me you use exfoliators to remove dead skin cells and other stuff that clogs up the pores.' This explanation had clearly been a good decision since clogged pores were quite a hot issue. They were all experimenting with make-up and there was some fear that they might be damaging their skin by 'spreading this goo all over it'. All of a sudden, the group was discussing their skin types, the products they had used in the past and how effective they were, how they were given trial samples and got information from magazines. How they felt when they had skin breakouts, huge zits before important dates, how periods affected their skin. The group was answering all the moderator's questions and she hadn't even got around to asking some of them yet!

Some time later the energy seemed to subside, and as she wanted to check she had all the information, the moderator asked them all to write down their skin type, their cleansing routine, the products they had used in the past and the ones they were using currently. She reviewed this with each respondent, again emphasising that everyone had different needs and opinions, and pulling out correlations between skincare needs and products: 'So you say your skin is sensitive, because it stings sometimes, is that right? And so, you use things that have the word "sensitive" on them? And you would expect those to be more ... gentle? Less harsh?'

But it was clear that product features were only part of the story. For one thing, they seemed to have an innate understanding of which products and brands were aimed at their age group, and which ones were for older, more sophisticated, girls. A quick mapping confirmed this. Her instructions were simple.

'Can you just group these together for me? In whatever groups you think they go together. It's entirely up to you. We can do this two or three times over if you don't agree the first time.'

Looking at the packs which the girls grouped and described as being aimed at 'spotty teenagers', and the ones which were 'like the ones you get in department stores' the moderator realised she was about to unlock some important insights.

First, she got the group to list the similarities in each category so she could understand what packaging cues were critical in signalling the type of user. She realised that 'spotty teenagers' was a stereotype judgement that applied to an out-group of teenagers (despite the fact that all the girls had experienced more than the occasional spot themselves). 'Tell me about a "spotty teenager"' the moderator said. 'What are they like? Where do they live? What do they do?'

As the description flowed, the moderator checked what the group meant by 'sad' and 'geeky' in this context. Then came a key question: 'So why is it important to not be like this?'

It seemed as if the advertising for these products had concentrated so much on the functional effectiveness of these products that they had acquired a desperation stigma. What the girls wanted was to be able to manage their skin problems, but to do so with aplomb and style. They had a vision, a fantasy, that older girls who had left school had money of their own, were discriminating and sophisticated and could therefore buy 'department store' products with more glamorous packaging and French descriptions. They did not want to dwell on their problems, they wanted to feel attractive and in control of their problems, and these older girls were their role models.

This was possibly the answer to the client's other main issue – what to do with the two new products they had developed. These were described on what the client called concept boards, but the moderator took pains to tell the group that this was just a way of showing them new ideas to discuss. After a diversion caused by confusing language on the boards, one of the products was agreed to have something good to offer – to three of the girls at least. Having acknowledged it would not suit everybody, the moderator had the group imagine these functional products in more sophisticated packaging. 'We'll just make it up for the moment,' she said. 'Just imagine this sort of pale green pack with that sort of silver writing, but it gets rid of your spots as effectively as any of those "spotty teenager" ones?'

They weren't sure. The energy level dropped. The moderator sensed a lack of interest or involvement. Something wasn't working here; perhaps her theory was wrong. 'Let's go back over this,' she said. 'Have I understood it right?' Yes, it was clear that the product had some credible functional attributes – they understood the ingredients – they would be interested in trying it. Yet, there was an issue about how to package and present it. 'You are definitely not keen on this packaging suggestion,' she noted. 'What is it that doesn't work for you?'

'It would look too much like something from – (she named a large store that sold their own skincare).'

'I'm not clear why that is a problem,' said the moderator.

'It would put people off.'

'I'm sorry, I still don't understand. It doesn't have to look exactly like that; I'm sure the designers would want to make it look different, and I would have thought it was the sort of place where people (like you) like to shop?'

'Yes, but ...' The respondent hesitated. The moderator thought she noticed some anxiety in her voice. Time to find out what was going on. 'I get the feeling you are bothered about something?' the moderator reflected.

All of a sudden, two or three girls burst out together.

'It's the women in there, the ones behind the counters. They are so snooty.'

'Yeah, and they always look at you like you are trying to steal something.'

'If you want to look at something in there they are always staring at you, like they are thinking "she's too young to be in here, she hasn't got enough money to buy this"'.

'And they never smile and say "hello, can I help you?"'

Now it made sense. The suggested packaging combination had triggered some very negative feelings about the very sort of products the girls were interested in. Time to delve deeper into this issue and hopefully come up with something constructive rather than just relaying the problem back to the client. As far as the moderator was aware, the client did not have fixed ideas about the packaging, as long as it had some key elements of the brand identity. The moderator had suspected that she might have to understand what the brand meant to them, what strengths it had and what were the key visual cues or signals that distinguished that brand. She had already learnt some of this from the mapping exercise, but she wanted to give her client firmer guidance on how the packaging should communicate both the product and brand values. She was ready with her 'toolkit' – literally a large bag with paper, colouring pens and a large selection of pictures and headlines clipped from newspapers and magazines.

'I have the feeling you know what sort of pack you want in your own mind, and I need to be able to see it and understand it myself, so perhaps you can use these to show me. I am sure you will be able to find some pictures that have the right colours or the image for the packaging, even if they are nothing to do with skincare at all. Just look quickly through these and see what jumps out at you,' she said, handing out a large and messy pile of clippings. She wanted the girls' intuition to be working now, not carefully considered judgement. Remembering that one of the girls had said at the beginning she was interested in art, the moderator offered another form of expression. 'I've got some colours and paper here, if anybody would like to draw or design their own ...'

The moderator chatted with the girls as they did their task, asking why some pictures were rejected while others were chosen, and finally it was time to review the findings. Two hours had almost flown by, and she needed to pull together some of the threads. The girls needed to be made aware that the group would finish soon too. Although they had seemed so diffident at first, they were now very involved and were laughing with each other at some of the pictures in the collection. The moderator raised her voice to take back control of the group. 'We are going to be finishing soon, so I will be asking you to tell me what you have picked here and why, and then we will summarise what has been covered in the group.'

As the girls laid out their pictures, some common themes began to emerge. A particular shade of light blue was picked out by two girls, and the others agreed it felt very clean, looked a bit more sophisticated, but wasn't a traditional skincare packaging colour. Touches of a Japanese theme emerged – the girls explaining that this seemed to be the beginning of a trend in fashion and cosmetics – while the girl who had done the drawing had chosen a bottle shape reminiscent of a well-known nail polish remover. This would send signals about the strength and effectives of the product as a cleanser, while the colours and design would suggest the gentleness and refinement they wanted from more sophisticated products, while keeping well away from any associations with 'snooty' sales assistants. It wasn't a professional job, but it would be helpful in briefing a designer – assuming similar principles emerged in the following groups.

The moderator started to go over what she had learnt, with the group interjecting when she missed a point or used the wrong phrase, but she was well aware that she still wanted to probe the 'trying on identity' issue. There was not much time left now, but it might become a more important section of the topic guide for the next group. So just as they were reviewing the collage exercise, the moderator asked whether they had found any pictures of people who they would like to be for an evening or a day? A quick sort through the mess and each respondent had at least two or three. 'Tell me about one of these people, what would you imagine it is like to be them?'

This was clearly quite a powerful question, and the moderator allowed each girl to talk for a few minutes before summarising the common themes that had emerged from the exercise. The moderator knew that a deeper exploration of this would produce some valuable results, but the client would want it all related to skincare product choices, so perhaps this was something for a further piece of exploratory research. So the moderator continued her overall summing up, and finished the group by asking the girls if there was anything else they wanted to say, or any questions they wanted to ask her. Although they said no, and began to troop out, one stayed behind and asked the moderator about how she had started in market research. This girl had found the discussion so interesting that she wanted to investigate research as a career option. She was sent away with some brief advice and the phone number of the Association for Qualitative Research. Meanwhile the moderator had ten minutes to clear up before the next group arrived ...

# The Nature of Qualitative Market Research Interviewing

This chapter describes the main characteristics of qualitative market research in relation to interviewing issues, and how it differs from academic qualitative research. It highlights some of the topics explored in more detail in later chapters. The evolution of qualitative market research has resulted in both a 'psychological legacy' and a craft-based profession that uses theory more implicitly than explicitly. A historical eclecticism allows commercial researchers to borrow and employ a wide range of ideas and techniques, working in new ways and employing explanations at different levels as and when they are useful to the client. Some of the more common interview formats and settings are outlined, as well as an overview of the strengths and limitations of interviewing as a data collection method.

## A NOTE ABOUT TERMINOLOGY

Interviewing in a group setting is referred to as moderating in this book, so an interviewer is described as a 'moderator' when in the context of a group. In much of the book, the skills described are relevant to both group and individual depth interviews, so the terms are used interchangeably. The term 'researcher' is also used, sometimes for variety, and sometimes to remind the reader that the interviewer or moderator will have been involved in the planning of the research, and will take a role in the analysis, interpretation and presentation. In the UK, a freelance researcher is likely to be involved in every aspect of the project, while a researcher working in a company may work as part of a team in which there is some division of labour.

It should be assumed that 'group' refers to all types of market research groups, unless otherwise specified. These will include focus groups, group discussions and the many variants that have evolved. The term 'respondent' covers participants in all types of interviews, and includes consumers, customers, employees, stakeholders, voters, supporters and service users.

The term 'unconscious' plays a major role throughout the book and has many shades of meaning. Researchers use it loosely in its naturalised form to mean intuitive, private, emotional and unaware content not easily available to consciousness; it is also discussed in a specifically Freudian and psychodynamic context. There is also the realm of information processing 'out of conscious awareness', and the concept of the 'hidden'. This refers mainly to that which is hidden in the assumptions of the cultural context and is 'unconscious' to the individual.

## SOURCES OF INFORMATION

This book is based on nearly 30 years of experience as a commercial research practitioner, conducting literally hundreds of groups each year. This is augmented by formal training in psychology, counselling, Neuro-Linguistic Programming (NLP) and organisational development, and over 15 years' experience of training others in qualitative research skills, particularly in interviewing. Over the years many research practitioners have shared both their skills and their difficulties in the context of such training and development. Many hours of watching people moderate, analysing and discussing the skills and the processes, have provided a firm grounding for developing the themes in this book. This experience has been complemented by the opportunity to watch experienced practitioners conduct groups on video, and interviews with researchers in the USA and UK, as well as those who work internationally.

## CHARACTERISTICS OF QUALITATIVE MARKET RESEARCH

Book 1 provides a full discussion of the characteristics of qualitative market research, but some are listed here to provide a context for interviewing skills and approaches that can differ significantly from those found in the academic context. In particular, the issues of researcher motivations, implicit and flexible use of theory and the need to work within the discipline of client objectives, are discussed below.

### Researcher Motivations

The issue of the researcher's motivation is very pertinent to interviewing, since to be done well it requires engagement and commitment. Academics may wonder what motivates commercial researchers to work for someone else – if there is anything apart from the money. Some commercial researchers are just doing a job, but many devote considerable time and energy to it. The work regularly involves long, unsocial hours, travel to unglamorous places, while the processes of analysis and reporting rarely fit into office hours. The money may be good, but it would take more to justify the demanding 'quallie lifestyle'.

Academic qualitative researchers are likely to be working with a research question which they own and are engaged with, that they have spent time considering and developing. In contrast, commercial researchers will be working with somebody else's questions and issues, and possibly only over a period of a few weeks. As Mike Imms and Gill Ereaut point out, the essential role of both types of researcher is similar – to mediate between the worlds of the question owners and those of the researched. However, a fundamental difference is that the commercial researcher has to simultaneously play the role of 'pure researcher' and 'business partner'. (See Book 1 for more details.) The pure researcher has to manage the processes of setting up, interviewing, analysing and reporting – usually within a narrow timescale and a specified budget. The business partner role is employed at the same time to keep in mind the interests of the client organisation. This distinction also helps explain the motivations of commercial researchers themselves. As pure researchers they have a deep curiosity about the lives and world-views of others; as business partners they get the chance to satisfy this curiosity while at the same time helping an organisation make better decisions. Qualitative market researchers accumulate detailed knowledge related to subjects they specialise in, and general knowledge about lifestyles, processes of consumption and the effectiveness of various research methodologies.

> You are educating yourself, going to different places, finding out all sorts of interesting things, and getting paid for it. (Moderator interview)

### Implicit and Flexible Use of Theory

Whereas academic researchers make explicit the theoretical framework they are using, qualitative market researchers tend not to do this unless it is specifically relevant to the methodology that will be employed (for example, in observational work, or interpreting results within a particular model such as Transactional Analysis or NLP – see Chapter 4 for more about these). Some clients take a great interest in methodology, while others trust the researcher to choose the best approach, and see methodology as a distraction from the findings. In some European countries, particularly France and Germany, there is a more overt use of theory, both psychoanalytic and sociological approaches having their supporters.

Whatever the researcher's background, the practice of qualitative market research is based on sound theoretical principles. Some researchers may not be aware of it, but the manner in which they design samples, set up, introduce and run groups has evolved as the best way of making the most of small group dynamics, while avoiding the pitfalls. As Chapter 5 explains, the standard group introduction given by the moderator is a powerful communication that enables the moderator to dissipate some respondent anxieties, start the forming process and establish norms and expectations for the group session. It also works against the forces that lead to conformity and groupthink, and starts to equalise power structures in the group – while retaining a measure of control for the moderator to deal with possible disruption later.

Similarly, styles of interviewing (often learnt through watching a more experienced practitioner) enable qualitative market researchers to keep the focus on the client's issues, while remaining within the respondent's frame of reference and using the interactions between respondents to explore the research questions. Having been taught listening and eliciting skills – whether formally or by 'osmosis' – it takes some effort to produce a poor interview within a qualitative market research framework. There are mistakes, but setbacks are usually recoverable, often because the group is aligned with the interviewer in wanting to help produce useful information. Lack of knowledge of the theoretical basis does not detract from successful application of the skills.

Another example of the implicit use of theory is the interview or topic guide, a framework for the approach to the interview that is agreed by researcher and client. There is a widely accepted method of developing topic guides, which utilises a few simple principles. Experimenting with different sequences and types of question allows researchers to establish what does and doesn't work in a topic guide. This practical knowledge is easily fitted into a more formal model. The Tuckman model (Chapter 4) helps explain why certain questions don't work early on; why the group sometimes feels easy and then goes into an awkward phase; or why respondents may not want to leave at the end.

Qualitative market researchers have short timescales, so they use additional techniques to help elicit relevant material. Whether or not they have heard of or believe in split-brain research, the psychoanalytic concept of projection or the idea that people process information in different modalities (see Chapters 3 and 4 for explanations), they will use visual and auditory material to stimulate discussion, and set respondents tasks that might involve pictures, music, drawing, imagining or even acting. These enable them to access other aspects and layers of respondents' experience, and to translate the intuitive, the emotional, the non-verbal and the hidden into concepts that can be verbalised in the interview situation. Many of these 'projective and enabling' techniques are directly borrowed from clinical practice and are embedded in particular theoretical approaches – but to the commercial researcher it is their usefulness in unlocking the research question that matters most.

There is a fluidity, flexibility and willingness to experiment with interviewing styles, techniques and methodologies that might be hampered within a more formal theoretical structure. As client questions and issues become ever-more demanding, qualitative market researchers employ a frontier spirit – a willingness to work with what is available, an ability to challenge rules and preconceptions, a search for the new and insightful. They may be unaware of the theory underlying the traditional forms of practice, but many are interested in learning about new concepts that could help in their work. Approaches such as NLP, semiotics and brico-lage all excite interest, but the researchers learning about these all have one main question – how can I use this effectively in my work?

Some researchers are deeply involved with a particular theoretical per-spective, and others have their preferences. Many have a lack of attach-ment to any perspective, understanding that different types of theory can be helpful at different times. Indeed one of the skills of the researcher is to identify the levels at which clients need explanation. Understanding why people enjoy bubbles in their chocolate might require explanations on physiological, emotional and symbolic levels; understanding what might motivate teenage girls towards higher education will involve looking at the cognitive, emotional, social and cultural. Researchers can move freely between levels and theories in one piece of work, should they choose to do so. The main restriction is whether the client finds it helpful.

### Disciplines of Qualitative Market Research

With the exception of those clients (such as advertising agency planners) who do their own research, qualitative market research practitioners are working towards somebody else's objectives. These need to be inter-nalised and kept as a constant reference point through the project, parti-cularly during the interviewing process. They provide the inner guidance on how to proceed when interviewing moves into unknown territory. The role of the researcher is that of mediator between two worlds – the world of the client and that of the respondent. Yet it is rarely possible for the researcher to fully immerse him or herself in the respondent's world – the client's needs and issues remain as a beacon throughout.

Most research projects have tightly defined boundaries – defined by what is relevant to the commissioning client. Researchers have the oppor-tunity to challenge and expand these, but more commonly have to main-tain these boundaries in interviewing by keeping respondents within a set of topics.

In addition, some projects may be tightly focused. For example, the research objectives may be as narrow as making minor changes to a brand logo – but these can have far-reaching implications. The researcher has to work with the logo, unpacking all the meanings and associations that surround the brand, but keeping it as the centre of the interviewing process.

Some research may go into a general bank of 'consumer insight', and many projects will directly or indirectly contribute to commercial deci-sions that involve the client spending large amounts of money. These decisions impact ultimately on the financial health of the organisation and the jobs of its workers. Researchers do bear some responsibility for the role they play in the influencing of these decisions.

## RESEARCH ISSUES AND METHODS OF ENQUIRY

There is a close relationship in qualitative research between the research issues and topics and the methods of enquiry used to illuminate them. Qualitative market research is framed by the needs of the client organisation – a topic covered in more detail in Book 1.

### Qualitative Market Research Issues

Some research projects may be regarded as basic. There may not be a need for much in-depth analysis or interpretation to decide which packaging variant communicates freshness best. Some clients have built up an extensive qualitative knowledge from a series of research projects, and do not need to have this repeated, although minor aspects of it will need to be updated. However, the role of qualitative market research is usually to go deeper, as the AQR, the UK industry body for commercial qualitative practitioners, implies:

> Qualitative research is a powerful, invaluable tool enabling marketers and other professions to explore people's motivations, behaviour, desires, and needs. (AQR website)

The key value that qualitative market research contributes is the understanding of the processes of motivations, desires and needs – which crucially, many consumers may not be fully aware of, or may not feel it is socially desirable to admit to. As the oft-quoted saying goes:

> People don't always say what they mean or mean what they say. (Sampson 1998)

The questions and issues for interviewing therefore involve various routes to developing understanding:

- Exploring individual experiences in detail, looking at the interaction of emotions, needs and behaviour.
- Understanding how respondents map the subject; what dimensions and connections are of importance to them.
- Dealing with sensitive subjects (and surprisingly, subjects that involve love or money may be more sensitive than subjects like haemorrhoid remedies).
- Finding ways of helping respondents verbalise what they know and will admit to.
- Making it safe to verbalise private things they might not like to admit to.
- Finding ways of expressing the intuitive, the non-verbal, that which is below the level of everyday consciousness.

- Facilitating creative and constructive reactions to new concepts and ideas.
- Understanding how the social context affects individual behaviour.
- Clarifying what assumptions are implicit, but are invisible because they are taken for granted.

These issues can be categorised as those mainly relevant to individual psychology, those that describe social influences, and those that are cultural; shared values embedded in the world-view of the respondent.

### A Typology of Qualitative Market Research Approaches

Different types of research require different approaches to interviewing. Variations in methodology do not work in practice as a basis for under-standing different types of qualitative research. Sykes and Brandon (1990) list a number of methodologies on offer, from focus groups to peer groups, family groups, sensitivity groups, commando groups, conflict groups, extended creativity groups and even behavioural modification groups. They also point out 'that there is generally little solid guidance as to which approach is to be preferred for a given application, and how it is best operationalised' (Sykes and Brandon 1990: 168).

For the purposes of understanding the different types of interview, a classification by research objectives makes most sense, as the objectives inform the approach to the whole project. Book 1 gives a more detailed view of the range of typical project objectives. These include the following.

- **Screening:** of concepts and vocabulary, usually as a prelude to quantitative research.
- **Exploration:** mapping out the nature and dynamics of a market, sub-culture or organisation; exploring and giving a coherent account of the status quo. It might include observational methods, mappings and other categorisation techniques, and is most likely to allow respondents to set the agenda. The key questions here are: What is the situation? Where are we? What is the nature of this market? What do people feel and believe in general? What is everyday life like in relation to our product or service?
- **Strategic development:** extending the 'exploratory' function to generate, refine and give direction to future strategic decisions. This might use creativity-enhancing techniques for idea generation, and forward-looking 'what if' approaches in interviewing.
- **Diagnostic assessment:** offering an explanation for a particular state of affairs, such as accounting for a change in the fortunes of a brand, or explaining puzzling findings from other information sources. The interviewer needs to have the mindset of a detective, checking and testing hypotheses, and is likely to have a high degree of control over the process.

- **Creative development:** this term often applies to a specific kind of project used especially in advertising development to help nurture creative ideas from rough to finished executions (see Wardle, Book 6). It can also apply to the development and refining of embryonic product or marketing ideas, especially where the potential of the underlying idea needs to be understood separately from the vehicle used to communicate it. The interviewing strategy is likely to contain some exploratory approaches followed by reactions to stimulus material that describes a range of options.
- **Evaluation:** assessing the value of a past action or the potential of a future action; judging the potential of new product, policy, or marketing ideas, for example. This is likely to be a blend of descriptive and diagnostic research, and will require the researcher to be particularly careful in questioning about memory of recent events and cautious in interpreting and disentangling possible causes and effects.

## QUALITATIVE MARKET RESEARCH AS A CRAFT-BASED PROFESSION

There are relatively few papers describing the paradigms or frameworks that qualitative market researchers use. A recent example, by Spackman, Barker and Nancarrow (2000), acknowledges that qualitative market research 'is essentially a craft-based profession, a profession that is largely pragmatic rather than theory and philosophy inspired' (p. 91). They go on to examine the major paradigms underpinning market research in general, the positivist and the phenomenological, and suggest there is an emerging paradigm of 'informed eclecticism' for the twenty-first century – 'a new way of positioning market research itself within the wider knowledge mix'.

The pragmatic approach of many qualitative market researchers and the sheer volume of work that they do, preclude all but a minority from taking a deep interest in such theoretical issues, although they quickly adopt any new techniques that appear. Commercial researchers accumulate a massive amount of practical field experience, whereas 'few academic researchers undertake more than one or two research projects in any year' (Catterall 2000). Nevertheless, in learning the craft, researchers do embrace a particular way of approaching their subject. Operating successfully as a qualitative market researcher requires the adoption of a qualitative 'mindset' – an approach characterised by certain beliefs and values.

### The Qualitative Mindset – Ways of Thinking and Experiencing in Research

The quality of a research interview is affected by the quality of the interviewer's presence – the extent to which they can give their attention fully to somebody else. This ability is perhaps best described as a qualitative way of *being*. It is possible to *know* all the theory of qualitative research and not be able to do it at all. It is also possible to *do* qualitative research by following the practices and guidelines and to do it well, but the most challenging projects require an engagement in the process at every level.

> I really believe there has to be the appropriate connection at any given time, with each individual in the room. And that is why I love this job, you have to care about them, you have to love them, you have to be at their level and they will open up and talk to you. (Moderator interview)

A major strength of qualitative market research is its ability to deal with creative materials (such as advertising and product concepts) as well as producing insights from the activities of everyday life. To achieve this, the interviewer needs to remain open-minded, to question assumptions, to listen with great sensitivity and to probe areas of incongruence, disconnection between stated attitudes and known behaviour, and discover new areas for investigation.

This requires versatility, an ability to be non-judgemental and enough self-awareness to be able to bracket (temporarily set aside) one's own preconceptions. Being able to think on your feet is also essential – and to cope with being watched by clients while doing it.

The researcher has to be keenly aware of the importance of emotion as an essential component of motivation and decision-making, and has to be willing to work with emotional issues. The interviewer needs to be alert to hearing mundane or everyday speech in new ways, to question and go beyond the obvious.

Interviewers pay careful attention to consumer language, to labels, descriptors and methods of categorising products and concepts. They have to be able to deal with the discomfort of working within the ambiguities this process can uncover. Respondents are often discovering what they think and feel about a subject as the interview progresses, and so do not present a consistently thought-out perspective. The qualitative way of thinking must be fluid and the interviewer prepared to change the nature of the questions that need to be asked. Interviewing provides the basic materials for analysis. It follows that the richer and more creative the interview, the more potential there is for making meaning in the analytical process.

One way of seeing the interviewing process is as stepping into the world of the respondent (as defined by the limits of the project), noting and mapping the cognitive, social, emotional and cultural landscape, and then returning to the research objectives of the client, with a translation of it into meaningful, coherent, actionable findings.

### Skills in Qualitative Market Research Interviewing

The qualitative approach relies on much more than asking open-ended questions and setting up topics for discussion. Later chapters will cover the skills in detail. They include:

- Eliciting information without asking too many direct questions, without leading or suggesting ideas to the respondent.
- Using honed listening skills to unlock the insights.
- Employing sensitivity to notice non-verbal indicators of emotional states, and probing appropriately.
- Creating enough trust and empathy for respondents to feel safe in expressing their private thoughts and feelings.
- Using non-verbal techniques such as music, images and actions to access the 'knowledge' people have stored as a series of impressions or feelings, to avoid premature rationalisation.
- Keeping people focused on narrowly defined objectives, maintaining interest and energy and exploring topics in different ways.
- Managing projects that have extensive social, environmental, or economic consequences – transport issues for example, maintaining the breadth of vision, while still providing the insights clients need.

In work with groups, the dynamics between the respondents provide creativity, shared understandings and individual differences, and yet can also be a source of tension and difficulty. This can silently undermine the research, unless the moderator knows how to notice and deal with it.

Interviewing is the most widely used method of data collection in qualitative market research. Researchers have found many ways of enhancing the interviewing process to generate the information they require; and in most market research projects, group interviews are the most cost-effective option. To many casual observers, research interviewing does not seem to require a great deal of skill. (Depth) interviewers or (group) moderators make it look easy and often enjoyable.

> 'Well … qualitative research is really easy … all it is chatting to a few people for an hour or so.' (Young advertising planner quoted in Gordon 1997)

The interview or group flows well, everybody contributes, insights appear, there is occasional laughter, and the whole endeavour seems to be a relatively effortless method of gathering rich and relevant data.

What is not so apparent is that the researcher is using him or herself as the research instrument, and is working simultaneously at the levels of content – dealing with the questions – and of process, actively building the interviewing relationship. In a feat of multi-level processing, the moderator is sensitive to the energy level of the group, to the personalities and needs of individual respondents, is listening deeply to what is being said (and what is not being said), and is developing new lines of questions based on rolling hypotheses developed from the information just obtained. These will be couched in the language respondents are comfortable with, although the objectives of the research will almost certainly have been phrased in marketing jargon. As one research trainee put it, 'Moderators are like ducks – everything looks smooth on the surface, but they are paddling furiously underneath.' While experienced moderators don't paddle quite so energetically, a great deal that goes on is not visible to an observer, as the story in the introductory chapter shows.

## INTERVIEW FORMATS AND SETTINGS

Book 1 gives more extensive descriptions of qualitative research methodologies. There are many different formats for the interviewing relationship: individual interviews (or 'one-on-one' in the USA), 'paired depths', groups of various sizes, one-off and reconvened or extended interviews, workshops, qualitative hall tests, panels, etc., which are sometimes given proprietary names by research companies. Every variable that can be manipulated has been experimented with. For example, research is usually conducted with current or potential users of a product or service, but it can be useful to work with lapsed users, non-rejectors, or users of competitive brands. Normally samples are structured so that groups have demographic or attitudinal commonalities – but a great deal can be learnt from 'conflict' groups, where the differences between people are revealing.

Some researchers use longer groups and interviews (3 hours or more) as part of a study, often if a number of projective and creativity techniques are to be used. Others establish on-going relationships with 'key informants' in order to be kept up-to-date with what is happening in a market.

Respondents can be asked to complete a diary, fulfil a creative task (such as finding three pictures that represent softness) or change their behaviour (stop having carbonated drinks, for example), before, after, or in between taking part in interviews. Workshops can last for a whole day, and involve the respondents being set several different tasks, interspersed with periods of discussion and reflection. Many researchers use their skills to offer facilitation of client groups, particularly brainstorming sessions. Observational studies are quite common, although these may be combined with a form of interview. They include accompanied shopping, trips to social venues and observation in public and work places. Use of the Internet in research is increasing; not just for moderating online groups, but for establishing dialogues with respondents and maintaining longer-term distance relationships for projects. (See Book 3 for a full description of non-interviewing methods.)

With such a choice of methods, and further opportunities for inventing their own, one of the skills researchers employ is the ability to deconstruct the client's objectives in terms of the methods that will produce the most appropriate material for analysing and interpreting the research.

### Individual and Group Interviews

In terms of interviewing skills and processes, the key distinction is between interviewing one individual in depth, and working with a group.

**Individual depth** interviews are used when groups would be impractical; the respondents are too busy or have a great deal of specialised knowledge, when following a process in depth and detail is important, when discretion is needed for a sensitive subject, and when it is possible that the respondent would be uncomfortable or adversely affected by a group situation. Depth interviews tend to be more expensive as they use up more resources for a smaller sample size. For specialised samples, recruitment costs are likely to be higher; there may be more travel involved between appointments, possibly the hire of several locations, and certainly much more of the researcher's time is involved both in interviewing and analysis. Although it is sometimes thought that they are easier to handle than groups, as there are no group dynamics to deal with, the relationship between interviewer and respondent comes into sharp relief. A depth interview offers greater opportunities for empathy and building rapport, but may be experienced by the respondent as more intrusive and self-revealing. Without the safety of a group, respondents can feel put on the spot. They have to answer all the questions – they can't just nod assent sometimes. Each answer has to be constructed from scratch rather than built up from other people's ideas. The focus is entirely on the respondent; there is no one to rescue them or deflect questions or comments. Should there be a mismatch in personality and style between interviewer and respondent it will become much more obvious than it would in a group. In their study of respondents' experiences of groups and depths, Gordon and Robson (1982) found that 'individual interviews are more stressful, and in practice more rigid and less open, than group discussions'. Some international researchers report that despite this, depth interviews are widely used in some European countries, particularly in Germany and the Netherlands.

A **group** setting always brings dynamics into play, arising from the processes of forming into a group and from the interactions of the respondents themselves. Groups can be more stimulating and creative through their interactions; they show social norms, shared understandings and individual perspectives. They are very good for establishing a range of opinion within a relatively short time. Some respondents find them less intimidating on the basis of safety in numbers, and they can be experienced as more entertaining – an important consideration for some respondents, and indeed some client viewers. However, the very dynamics that provide the benefits of the group interaction can come to undermine the quality of the information. Respondents can be covertly influenced by social norms, roles adopted by group members stop them responding authentically and interactions can run out of control – unless the moderator is sensitive to process as well as content.

The 1996 ESOMAR study of the European Market Research Industry expenditure (quoted in the Appendix to Gordon 1999) shows the preponderance of groups as the favoured data collection method in most European countries (except the Netherlands). Groups are cost-effective, and entertaining and involving for clients. The group has become a standard unit for costing and invoicing qualitative research.

## Normative and Creative Methodologies

In practice, much research in Europe is conducted in 'standard groups'. These consist of six to eight respondents, recruited to be a fairly homogenous sample, for a group lasting 1½ or 2 hours. As Chapter 4 shows, this format has evolved to minimise the potential biases of working in groups, and has stood the test of time. However, even a 'standard group' implies a wide range of techniques, and may be altered or adapted if researchers discover a better approach through their work in the field.

Methodological inventiveness is encouraged, especially at the proposal stage, where it can give a company a competitive edge. An example of methodological creativity was the development of 'Turnstile Groups' by MBL for studying perceptions of the elderly consumer. These involved researchers talking to groups of younger consumers in viewing facilities, while being observed by a group of older respondents, who were then interviewed in turn, enabling a more rounded picture of the different perspectives held by each age group. (These are also described in Europe as bifocal groups – Franzen and Bouwman 2001.)

Standard groups are more likely to be used for the more basic, undemanding research projects. They may be building on a bank of existing knowledge, assessing relatively minor changes or proposals, and may not require in-depth analysis. However, the changing commercial and media environment, the challenges of working within organisations as well as outside them, and the constant demand for innovation, mean that qualitative researchers are always looking for new ways of obtaining the information they need.

## Key Methodological Differences Between the USA and the UK

Mary Goodyear makes a distinction between cognitive style groups, which are more concerned with external information, and conative groups, which are more focused on inner feelings (Book 1 gives a detailed description of the differences). Goodyear describes the American tradition as largely cognitive. Group sizes tend to be larger (up to ten respondents) and the questioning style and procedure tend to be very structured.

> They are, indeed, groups 'focused' on specific issues with all the disciplines that follow from convergent thinking and control. The analysis or articulation of the problem has been worked on before, and so the interview is largely a question of confirming or expanding known issues. (Goodyear 1996: 345)

The role of the moderator is mainly to ask the questions the client specifies – in the order the client decides. There may be little or no analysis – since the questions are highly structured, the clients who are viewing feel they are getting the answers they need. The clients can become involved in the group process, directing the moderator to ask certain questions of certain people. Clients used to send in notes; nowadays the moderator may wear a headset or read from a screen to get the client questions directly before repeating them to the group.

Gill Ereaut (personal communication) points out that there is a different skill set for 'cognitive style' moderating. This 'show and tell' style is more akin to a skilled professional newsreader, who has to be able to present issues tailored to specific audiences and think on their feet, whereas the European style moderator is more like a journalist who is involved in all the information-gathering, and who has to make sense of the story as well.

However, it appears that this style of research co-exists with the conative approach in the USA. Some American researchers feel the cognitive approach is not as widespread as is thought:

> Re the perception that USA moderators are 'mouthpieces', my fellow QRCA[1] members and I also do not fully understand how this image became so pervasive. It's not the case with my colleagues. (Personal communication from H. Grace Fuller, Executive Director, RIVA Training Institute)

The European model of moderating, Goodyear says, 'assumes a different intellectual starting point, one that emphasises exploration, with the analysis taking place during and after the group' (Goodyear 1996: 345). The moderator may well be the researcher who has overall responsibility for designing, carrying and analysing the project. If not, the moderator will be part of a closely functioning team. This team is able to explore and make interpretations in the analysis, rather than just reporting what was said. European clients are more likely to accept the recommendations of the researcher, whereas US clients may want more control over the process.

International researchers who have observed groups in both continents note that Americans of all socioeconomic groups tend to be more expressive and more direct. European responses may sometimes need decoding, as when somebody gives praise without conviction; Americans are less likely to fall back on social niceties. In a paper given to the International section of the Market Research Society, Chrzanowska and Du Broff (1988) described a range of sociocultural and historical developments in the USA that have led to such differences. The higher rate of physical mobility in the USA created a need to quickly build bonds with others and to integrate into new groups. The Calvinist work ethic saw the rewards of success as signs of moral virtue, so Americans were not inhibited from discussing financial and consumer matters in a manner that might be distasteful to traditional British sensibilities. Many immigrants had cut their family ties, so social mobility depended more on money and consumer goods than the subtler signals of status that had evolved in Europe. Cognitive style groups might result in less useful information if they were carried out in the UK, but in the American setting they clearly offer information that is as rich and accurate as is required.

### European Variations

In international qualitative market research, groups and interviews in a number of countries are usually coordinated by the lead company. It is usual practice to use local moderators who are fluent in the language and customs of their country, with the groups often being observed by one of the coordinators. This has led to widespread usage of viewing facilities for such work, with many local companies owning their own studio. There is also some pressure for standardisation of moderating styles and techniques, to enable inter-country comparisons to be made. Coordinators believe that with the right training (of the moderator) and the right approach, most people in most countries can be persuaded to take part in the same techniques. Indeed, international research companies may seek to develop research materials that have cross-cultural validity. (A notable paper on this topic is 'Standardisation through creative expression: Projective techniques in international market research', by Alan Branthwaite 1995.)

Peter Cooper also addresses this issue and describes some international differences in approach:

> Within European countries there are also differences in attitudes and practice of Qualitative research. Northern Europeans are more reserved and require deeper probing. Southern Europeans are more open and playful. Americans are more verbal. (Cooper 1990: 127)

International researchers are reluctant to generalise, as they don't like to fall back into superficial stereotypes. However they tend to agree that Spanish and Italians have very lively groups, with relatively little warm-up, and moderators who need to stop several people talking all at once. Germans are found to be more formal and literal; moderators have more success with rating and ranking tasks than with more creative techniques, although the latter are possible. French moderators are prepared to be creative, philosophical and psychological, and left to their own devices might do fewer groups, but much longer ones. Scandinavians do take longer to warm up, and the British have a reputation for being more reticent than Southern Europeans.

## STRENGTHS AND LIMITATIONS OF QUALITATIVE INTERVIEWING AS A DATA COLLECTION METHOD

### Strengths

Qualitative interviewing allows people to tell their own stories in their own words – as long as the research framework is not too directive. What they choose to say and how they say it, gives a sense of their priorities and frames of reference. The interviewer can come to understand experiences and reconstruct events he or she has never taken part in, learn about different ways of experiencing the world and get insights into other people's categories, definitions, needs and desires. It is the perfect profession for the naturally curious.

Although interviewing is a social context with its own rules, interviewing is not too far removed from ordinary conversation; using similar cues for speaking and answering questions. While there is some anxiety amongst first-time interviewees, respondents mostly enjoy being the focus of attention and feel valued. They are therefore helpful, and once trust has been built, are willing to share thoughts and feelings they may not have spoken before.

The interview itself, and some of the techniques used in qualitative market research, give respondents insights about themselves; insights about products and communication issues and how others behave, so participating in the interview is regarded as informative. In a society where people are communicated *to* all the time, respondents appreciate the chance to talk back, knowing their views hold some influence.

People spend much of their time in group settings – family groups, educational classes, peer groups, social groups, work teams – so most are comfortable with a group interview, once specific details have been explained.

Although topic guides are used, qualitative interviewing is usually open enough to discover new areas to explore. Interviews can build upon knowledge, ideas and hypotheses from earlier interviews, allowing full exploration of the issues. At the same time, it can be direct and efficient in gathering the required information. Group interviews are particularly cost-efficient when a range of opinions is required.

In a comparison between group discussions, accompanied shopping preceded by individual interviews, and in-home participant observation on toilet cleaning, Pike and Gordon found that 'the main strength of the group discussion methodology lies in the arena of the emotions, which could be placed in the broad social, cultural and psychological values of the target market'.

> The very fact that women were released from the real context of home and toilet allowed participants to share with each other and bring to the surface feelings that had remained hidden before ... (Quoted in Gordon 1999: 100)

## Limitations

The same comparison showed that the ethnographic method (in this case video-recording the process of toilet cleaning combined with respondent explanations) was able to release personal insights and explanations that do not occur out of context. 'Through the enactment of behaviour, the individual is able to access thoughts and emotions that are not accessible via other research models' (Gordon 1999: 99).

There may be a gap between respondents' perceptions and explanations, and what happens in observable reality. The respondent's self-image may not match the reality of their behaviour, or they may have blind spots which influence behaviour, but in a manner unseen by the respondent.

In the consumer realm, there are habitual behaviours that are unlikely to be expressed in the interview, either because they seem utterly insignificant, or because they are outside the awareness of the respondent. In researching dieting, one meets respondents who genuinely believe they 'eat nothing all day' and still manage to gain weight. Respondents forget, ignore and re-frame what they do eat, leaving a puzzled interviewer trying to work it out.

The social context of interviewing leaves the respondent open to influences from the interviewer, and in a group, from other respondents. Interviewers can become aware of their own judgemental positions and biases and try to set them aside (a process known as bracketing),[2] but commercial researchers rarely practise this. Bracketing does not deal with respondents who may present themselves in the most positive light and try to impress or outdo each other. There is an element of social theatre that is not always immediately obvious to the moderator. Nor is this 'impression management' always predictably positive – some groups will compete to show how lazy, irresponsible or uncaring they are – if these are the values espoused by their social reference group. Fare dodgers on public transport re-frame their 'deviant' behaviour as subverting an unfair system. While this provides a lot of useful information about the social and cultural context, it can leave the researcher unclear about the actual motivations and behaviour of individuals.

A final point is that the sociological/cultural studies perspective has challenged the status of language itself. Seale (1998) points out the language used by respondents can be seen either as a *resource* (which assumes there is a stable external reality independent of the language, and therefore respondents' accounts are real and authentic), or as a *topic*. In the latter case, language has no reliable relationship to any external reality – it is only reflective of the context in which it was produced. It is interesting as a 'situated account', but it is a version of their experience rather than an inalienable truth. Respondents' accounts are influenced by social values and ideologies they themselves are unaware of.

Although interviewing is only able to present a partial and limited view, mediated by language and social expectations, it remains the method of choice for most commercial researchers, who have evolved techniques for limiting the disadvantages of the method while enhancing its strengths.

## CONCLUSION

Spackman, Barker and Nancarrow (2000) describe their view of a new paradigm for the market research industry (both qualitative and quantitative) as 'informed eclecticism'.

> So the paradigm which is emerging ... is all about looking beyond research, drawing from disciplines and worlds outside research (from the classical areas of psychology and marketing to business studies, cultural analysis and sociology etc.) and doing this in a creatively eclectic, but sensible way. This is what we mean by Informed Eclecticism. (2000: 99)

In qualitative market research interviewing (and analysis) the eclecticism is already in evidence; the implicit use of a range of both major and minor theories being apparent. However, the next step is to make the eclecticism more informed. To meet the challenges set by their clients, researchers will need to choose approaches and techniques in interviewing with a greater awareness of their theoretical origins, their assumptions and implications. (See Chapter 9 for a further discussion of this.)

### KEY POINTS

- Qualitative market researchers vary in the extent to which they make explicit the theoretical frameworks that inform their work. They are judged on effectiveness in providing insights and information relevant to client needs, and have been creative and eclectic in meeting ever more demanding and varied client requirements.
- The role of qualitative market research is to explore the processes of people's motivations, desires and needs, and in order to do this it has to deal with the private, intuitive and symbolic world of the individual which is not readily accessible to consciousness.
- In interviewing, qualitative market researchers seek insight

  o  at an individual psychological level;
  o  at an interactive social level; and
  o  at a shared-meaning cultural level.

- The theory is not often made explicit by researchers themselves, although it is embedded in the mindset and the craft skills used by interviewers and moderators:

- o remaining open-minded, sensitive and non-judgemental while staying task-focused;
- o being aware that the interviewer him or herself is the research tool;
- o working with groups in ways that manage process issues;
- o eliciting information in ways that minimise the drawbacks of interviewing;
- o using additional techniques that maximise the creativity, depth and relevance of research information.

- Commercial researchers may be motivated partly by money; but as 'pure researchers', they have the satisfaction of running effective research projects and satisfying their curiosity about other people's lives. They are simultaneously 'business partners' to their clients and have the satisfaction of helping them make better decisions.
- Interviewing is the most commonly used method of data collection. It is a direct and effective method of gathering data, and qualitative interviewing allows respondents to describe their world in their own terms.
- In Europe and the USA group methodologies are more commonly used than individual interviews, and 'the group' has become a convenient unit of qualitative research.
- Researchers are aware of the limitations of interviewing as a method of data collection. Where possible, they use techniques to extend the boundaries of interviewing, but will also use non-interviewing methodologies where appropriate.
- Researchers' lack of attachment to theories may be a factor in their willingness to be creative; to try new methods and techniques. Client needs stimulate methodological creativity, and the new challenge is to move into a more informed eclectic approach.

## NOTES

1 QRCA is the Qualitative Research Consultants Association in the USA and the RIVA Institute is one of the major qualitative research training institutions.
2 The phenomenologist Husserl advocated bracketing – setting aside preconceived notions – to enable one to objectively describe the phenomena under study. A description of the process can be found in part 15 of C. George Boeree's online text on Qualitative Methods (1998).

# Implicit and Explicit Theories about what Qualitative Market Research Interviewing Can Discover

The theory section in this book has been divided into two chapters. This one covers the theories about the nature of the information that qualitative market research can access – the content; Chapter 4 covers theories that relate more to the processes of research, focusing on interviewing. Both chapters aim to show how these theories have influenced the world-view and practice of commercial researchers.

This chapter covers concepts relating to the psychoanalytic, psychodynamic and the unconscious, showing how they have influenced thinking within qualitative market research. Influences from Humanistic and social psychology are equally embedded in the attitudes and beliefs researchers hold about interviewing relationships. These theories are sometimes used explicitly by researchers, as are others, both major and minor.

## WHAT DO QUALITATIVE RESEARCHERS AIM TO LEARN FROM INTERVIEWING?

Good definitions of qualitative market research are rare in the literature, and researchers often have to describe to their clients what they do in their own words. Here are a few excerpts from UK qualitative researchers describing what they feel is the aim of the interviewing process.

> Exploring their views, finding out in detail what they think about things they have never thought about before.

> Looking at their emotions, it's more about going down into the feelings, the irrational part.

> It's about insights, learning things that are not obvious. Qual goes deeper into what influences them.

They use words like 'uncover, explore, assess, look closely at, go down into, go deeper', which suggest that they are expecting to find and work

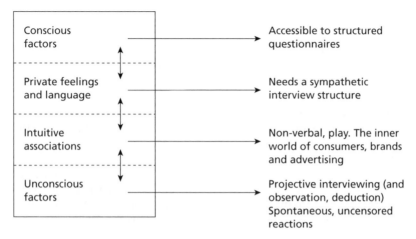

FIGURE 3.1   ***Researching symbolic attitudes to advertising: basic model*
(after Lannon and Cooper 1983)**

with much more than surface responses, the initial reasons or rationalisations that respondents might give when talking about their behaviour. There is an assumption that if research simply reports what people have said then it is not very good, it is shallow 'reportage'. Most researchers will probably have come across a 'layers of consciousness' model such as the one reproduced in Figure 3.1 from 'Humanistic Advertising' by Lannon and Cooper (1983: 203).

This model uses concepts such as 'private' and 'unconscious' in a naturalised manner. It draws from several theories and applies them in a manner calculated to make sense to an audience that may not be familiar with them. It is often at this sort of level that theory may make an appearance in qualitative market research.

It is not necessary to be familiar with the theory to be an excellent interviewer, group moderator and researcher, but it does give additional insights and other ways of looking at things. Some researchers may wish to identify themselves with a particular theoretical perspective, but many appreciate that there is no one unique truth about human nature, and seek the theories that have the most explanatory power for the circumstances.

### INFLUENCES ON THE DEVELOPMENT OF QUALITATIVE MARKET RESEARCH

Qualitative market research has an intriguing history, which is described more fully in Book 1 of this series. The evolution of commercial research is mentioned briefly here to make two main points:

- that it developed along a separate path from qualitative research in the social sciences;
- that early research was dominated by a psychoanalytic approach, which was discredited, but has left a 'psychological legacy', which is now taken for granted by many practitioners.

'Motivation research', research into the needs, emotions and motivations of customers, developed into a major movement in the USA in the 1950s.

> Historically, motivation research represents the first serious and systematic attempt to apply psychology to marketing at a time when marketing was dominated by economic thinking. In fact, motivation research had a very persuasive argument in the fact that consumers often did not behave logically as presumed by the economists but rather psychologically. (Sheth 1973)

Dr Ernest Dichter, a trained Freudian psychoanalyst, set up the first major institute of 'motivation research' in the USA, with an impressive blue chip client list (Imms 1999). According to Packard (1957), by 1954, there were 82 US companies claiming to conduct motivational research, in a directory published by the Advertising Research Foundation (ARF). The ARF described techniques such as 'group interviewing sessions', and the role of 'social psychologists' in guiding studies. It acknowledged the contribution of the Humanistic psychologist Carl Rogers in providing a 'non-directive' framework for research interviewing. Vance Packard (1957) provides some colourful descriptions of the depth interviewing techniques in use at the time.

There was eventually a backlash from quantitative researchers, as well as from some clients who thought it had been taken to extremes: 'They are attempting to prove that sales are controlled by the libido or that people buy merchandise because subconsciously they hate their fathers' (quoted in Packard 1957: 197). Motivational research became discredited in the USA. The psychoanalytic tradition tends to be diagnostic and prescriptive, an attitude which did not play well with some clients. Dichter gained a reputation for offering his own hypotheses with little evidence, and some clients became sceptical and suspicious. (Imms (1999) notes that this may be a reason why some current US practice limits the role of moderator, allowing clients to observe groups and make their own interpretations.) Vance Packard himself contributed to the decline of motivational research by causing a national outcry over 'the depth manipulators ... [who] ... try to invade the privacy of our minds' (1957: 216).

A subsidiary of Dichter's company was set up in the UK and was run by Bill Schlackman, before he in turn set up his own company, William Schlackman Limited, in 1961. Most of the early practitioners were psychologists not psychoanalysts; there was less of a tendency to make dramatic and unsubstantiated interpretations, and the excesses of the USA were avoided. Schlackman's became the unofficial training ground for qualitative market researchers, producing many figures who went on to shape the industry in later decades. Wendy Gordon describes how Bill Schlackman believed Dichter had over-sold motivational research, and how Schlackman taught her 'the fundamentals of human psychology applied to marketing research' (Gordon 1999).

The label 'motivation research' was gradually phased out and it evolved into a research approach with a 'psychological legacy' (Imms 1999). This retained some of the key ideas of psychoanalysis, such as the concept of unconscious, irrational and emotional influencing ideas. However, the language changed to avoid specifically Freudian concepts like repression and the Oedipus complex, into more of a discussion of the private, intuitive and symbolic world of the individual. There were also influences from other branches of psychology, notably Humanistic, so that qualitative market research today is a blending of a number of theoretical bases.

The aims of qualitative market research are still to explore consumer's motivations and behaviour, their desires and needs, but there are now many more frameworks for this, including cultural analysis.

> We understand the world and its meanings through cultural assumptions, shared meaning systems and taken-for-granted beliefs and values that are ideologically based and culturally reinforced. (Valentine 1996: 98)

As Valentine writes, 'our interpretive role is not to look for "truth"; but to crack the code [of meaning]' (Valentine 1996: 98). As the trend guru Faith Popcorn (1991) put it, sometimes the deepest truths can be found in the clichés of the culture.

The evolution of qualitative market research was also affected by changes in client requirements. The development of account planning in UK advertising challenged qualitative research agencies to provide much more sensitive and insightful work into brands and advertising communications. More sources of consumer data and the accompanying information overload mean client 'insight managers' are looking for understanding and integration as well as new ideas. The evolution of qualitative market research continues, with the increasing use of workshops involving clients and consumers, online research, non-interviewing methodologies (described in Book 3), and client involvement, in what has been re-conceptualised as a joint 'learning journey' (Trevaskis 2000: 275).

## THE IMPLICIT ROLE OF PSYCHOANALYSIS AND THE PSYCHODYNAMIC APPROACH

Even though 'motivational research' became discredited in America, it created the expectation that the proper role of qualitative market research was to give insights into 'hidden' factors that influenced human behaviour. This was perpetuated by practitioners seeking to distance themselves from quantitative research and to establish the value of commercial qualitative research to clients.

To learn more about the psychoanalytic heritage Freud has to be discussed, as he is the key figure in psychoanalysis. Freud developed and popularised the concept of the unconscious – an immense and ground-breaking achievement. It is hard to appreciate how much Freud changed Western understanding of the personality. Prior theories were rigid, seeing personality as a set of more or less immutable characteristics, and failing to address the richness of subjective experience, or account for dreams, passions, neuroses and violence, other than in a simplistic manner.

Other figures in the movement should be given credit too. Carl Gustav Jung collaborated with Freud but his interests in anthropology, and mythology led him to develop a different direction. His work on personality types forms the basis of the much-used Myers Briggs Type Indicator. Further breakaways included Adler, who saw hopes and ambitions, parental relationships and the social environment as important factors in healthy personality development. Otto Rank thought it was necessary to look at how societies shaped the consciousness of individuals within them. Karen Horney looked at anxiety, and strategies for reducing it as a critical factor, while Erik Erikson assessed the main psychological tasks the individual must complete at various life stages. These theories are of much potential value but are less well known. In a rare example, Jungian ideas about archetypes formed the basis of two papers given at the Market Research Society Conference 2000 (Cooper and Patterson 2000; Pawle 2000).

Both Freud and Jung have been attacked and to some extent discredited both in academic discourse and in popular books like *Against Therapy* (Masson 1990) and *The Jung Cult* (Noll 1996). To many researchers and clients, Freudian ideas are the old 'residual codes', that is, symbols of a way of thinking that has now been updated and surpassed. Few people understand the ideas in depth and many find the concepts laughable. As one UK researcher put it:

> You don't think of Freud as relevant any more; all this business about seeing everything as a sexual symbol – that is about the level of most teenage boys nowadays.

However, this has not stopped key concepts entering common usage. Far from being an outdated laughing stock, Freudian and psychoanalytic thinking is embedded in our culture and our popular ideas about psychological explanations. One of the most influential concepts is that of the unconscious.

## The Unconscious

Freud defined the unconscious as all the aspects of the psyche not available to awareness; it is inferred from observable phenomena. It holds suppressed and repressed emotionally charged memories and ideas. These 'ideas' can come from any source, including our own wishes, but are 'defended against' because they are not acceptable to the conscious mind (as shaped by the rules and expectations of society). Freud believed that unconscious ideas with strong emotional charges strive for expression in any way that they can – through physical symptoms, artwork, dreams, slips of the tongue and through our spontaneous behaviour (both 'normal' and neurotic). This gives a way of accessing the unconscious, which cannot be known directly. He realised that bringing these ideas to consciousness was a method of healing, and developed the 'talking cure'. Word association, still widely used in qualitative market research, was an important part of this process.

Many researchers would disagree with the emphasis Freud placed on the primacy and (largely sexual) nature of unconscious motivations. Ideas that might be acceptable in Freudian therapy are not necessarily useful in qualitative research. There are difficulties in reaching conclusions that are actionable in marketing terms. For example, a UK study allegedly concluded that the Space Hopper (a large ball on which children can sit and bounce along) offered 'an acceptable masturbatory opportunity', while a French recommendation that First Class on an airline should represent a return to the womb left the marketing team rather short of practical ideas. Although the reductionist Freudian approach may no longer be as helpful as it was to Ernest Dichter's early clients, other aspects of the theory still provide useful and valuable ways of thinking.

### The Structure of the Psyche

Freud used the concepts of divisions between various parts of the self to explain how unconscious motivations interacted with other aspects of the personality. He divided the self into the Id (unconscious instincts and drives), the Ego (the conscious self) and the Superego (the moral and social conscience).

The **Id** translates the organism's needs into drives or wishes, which ensure that all physiological needs are met. It works according to the pleasure principle ('I want it and I want it now') and is entirely selfish. Think of a child screaming blue murder for something and you have the Id. The Id also underlies primary process thinking – child-like wish fulfilment thinking. Some consumer product categories, such as small personal indulgences, seem to operate on this principle.

As an infant develops, a small part of the Id begins to realise that it has to work according to the reality principle: 'I can take care of my needs when I have the appropriate objects and circumstances.' This becomes the conscious **Ego**, the problem-solver, the mediator between desires and reality.

Freud viewed all human thought as a conflict or compromise between the pleasure principle and the reality principle, and saw much behaviour as a reduction of the tension between the two. Interviewers who have listened to someone talking of the complex factors involved in making a major purchase such as a car will recognise this description.

The experiences of the Ego in negotiating the difficulties of life (including dealing with the Oedipal conflict) become internalised as the **Superego**. An internalisation of punishments and warnings becomes the conscience (the shoulds and oughts) and rewards and positive models are internalised as an Ego Ideal. It is no coincidence that consumer and organisational cultures present people with *models* for appearance and behaviour, hoping these will become internalised standards for behaviour.

Freud's view of the psyche is amusingly summed up by the description of 'A maiden aunt and a sex-crazed monkey, locked in mortal combat in a cellar, refereed by a rather nervous bank clerk' (source unknown).

### Meeting the Id, Ego and Superego in Research

Despite the archaic and specialised use of language, once these concepts are understood they can become very pertinent. Returning to the example of dieting, respondents give very clear descriptions of primary process Id thinking when they describe how they succumb to 'forbidden foods' (itself an interesting concept). Their battles for control of their eating patterns are Ego battles, mediating between desires and reality, while it is the Ego Ideal they have internalised that is telling them they should lose weight. The theory immediately provides a model – a way of working with the contradictory dimensions and conflicts experienced by consumers. It suggests types of question that might be asked, interactions between different thought processes, and points at which interventions might be made to resolve the situation.

### Psychodynamic Theory

Psychodynamic theory is a broader derivation from psychoanalysis that has retained credence. It arose as a way of seeking integration between variants of psychoanalytic theory, and elements of it can be found in many current theories, from Transactional Analysis, to Family Systems to NLP. Psychodynamic theory has three common themes:

- As a result of upbringing, trauma, social expectations, etc., the psyche is split into different parts (which can be named and defined in many ways, from 'unconscious' to 'sub-personalities').
- These different parts have different agendas and so conflict arises.
- The conscious part of the mind is not fully aware of these deeper dynamics but they influence attitudes and behaviour.

Note, for example, that the Tuckman model of group processes (its use for researchers is described in Chapter 4) implies that the group is influenced by needs and desires that individuals are not fully conscious of. There is a constant dynamic between the need to be accepted as a full member of the group, and the need to be recognised as a unique individual, but few respondents would report this as their experience of a group process.

## Defence Mechanisms and Projective Techniques in Qualitative Market Research

There are other concepts used by qualitative market researchers that have roots in the psychodynamic approach. 'He is in denial about it', 'they could really identify with that image', 'when out drinking they regressed to the level of 10-year-olds' – these are common parlance nowadays but refer to specific mechanisms (in Freud-speak) developed by the Ego to protect itself from the 'lawless mob of instinctual urges' and the demands of the 'harsh moralist' Superego.

Some of these defence mechanisms operate internally. **Denial** (usually temporary), **repression** (motivated forgetting) and **suppression** may be evident to an analyst who knows the person well, but are unlikely to be clear to an interviewer.

However, some operate by externalising the unconscious 'idea', and expressing it in the outside world. This describes a key mechanism that has given its name to a broad raft of techniques used in interviewing – **projection**. The unacceptable idea is disowned by projecting it onto somebody or something else. This powerful mechanism may be responsible for prejudices and racist attitudes, as it can operate on a national and cultural as well as an individual scale. Qualitative market research makes use of projection, in different ways and with a lighter touch. For example, respondents 'project' a personality onto a brand from their intuitive accumulated knowledge of the brand. Chapter 8 gives a broad description of some common projective techniques such as personification. Freud even said that people needed to personify what they needed to understand!

**Identification** is the process of adopting somebody else's personality characteristics as one's own, and it happens constantly on a minor scale, as well as more dramatically, as when a child identifies with, or introjects, a missing parent. Identification is an important mechanism in advertising and communication of all types. People take more notice of a message if it offers something they intuitively feel may be missing from their lives. People identify with, and internalise, the values of models, celebrities and public figures. Interviewers deconstruct the process by finding out whom respondents admire and what values they share.

Some defence mechanisms appear as explanations of consumer psychology or are met by moderators as 'difficult' respondent behaviours. These include:

- **Fixation:** the Ego becomes fixed at a certain level of development instead of progressing further. Some explanations of smoking behaviour allude to it as an oral fixation.
- **Regression:** reverting to an earlier form of behaviour when under stress or threat. This often manifests either as outbursts or sulks, and produces a type of 'difficult' respondent that is hard to deal with. Faith Popcorn developed the concept of 'cocooning' (consumers' need for a secure home base), which is a form of regression (1991).
- **Intellectualisation:** when the emotion is stripped from a difficult or threatening idea, and it is treated as an intellectual curiosity. Such respondents avoid any mention of the emotional whatsoever.
- **Reaction formation:** developing a pattern of behaviour which is the direct opposite of the unwanted impulses or desires, e.g. becoming puritanical or moralistic. A lighter form of this sometimes encountered in interviews is 'polarity responding' – the person who is determined to do the opposite of what is required.

## SOCIAL PSYCHOLOGY

Social psychology is another body of theory that has had a mainly implicit role in qualitative market research. Psychoanalysis does situate the individual in the context of family and social relationships, but not very overtly. Social psychologists have pointed out that human beings are dependent on others for their very survival (in the early years of life) and are therefore supremely adapted for sociability. The concept of the 'looking glass self' was put forward by Cooley in the early 1900s, who wanted to explain that we judge ourselves not just by our own standards, but also by how other people respond to us and treat us. This idea developed into the concept of self-esteem. Mead (1934) said that the attitudes and values of significant others as well as society in general are internalised and form the basis for a 'generalised other' by which we judge ourselves. Situations where people can calibrate themselves against others of similar age and background (such as a group discussion) therefore provide useful information for respondents to compare themselves with their peers. Another aspect of social psychology is social identity theory. Henri Tajfel (1981) looked at human beings as members of social groups. These are not just peer groups but could include Volvo drivers, golfers, classical music appreciators and qualitative researchers – any group that has a distinct identity. Membership contributes to personal identity and to self-esteem, so people need to feel positive about the groups they belong to. If they sense that a group has little status in the eyes of others, they might try to distance themselves from it, or they may emphasise their belonging to a socially positive group. The idea of in-groups and out-groups can hardly be avoided in any work with teenagers. It is a short step to the concept of 'badge brands' that act as indicators of belonging to specific groups, and social identity theory underpins the qualitative investigation of 'user groups'. 'What kind of person would use this brand of aftershave, and how would he differ from a user of that one?'

Qualitative research groups often bring to light social factors simply through respondent interaction. Moderators learn to notice when socially significant comments are being made. There is a great deal more theory in social research, some of which – small group processes and dynamics – is covered in Chapter 4.

## THE INFLUENCE OF THE HUMANISTIC MOVEMENT

Humanistic psychology is sometimes called the human potential or personal growth movement, as it places emphasis on personal and social development. Its revolutionary holistic vision of the human being is far removed from the essentially psychopathological view of the psychoanalysts and the denial of conscious experience espoused by the other main school of psychology, the Behaviourists.

The overall label of Humanistic psychology now covers a wide range of approaches, from Gestalt, to Maslow's Hierarchy of Needs, to Transactional Analysis – to name the ones most familiar to qualitative market researchers. (Despite the term 'Humanistic', it does not exclude the spiritual.) The individual is seen as connected with others, as part of a network of interaction, which helps people make sense of the world. Indeed, creating a meaningful life is assumed to be one of the highest motivators for human beings – with the understanding that what is meaningful may well differ for each person.

Some aspects of Humanistic psychology deal with 'Bodywork' (exercises and awareness of the physical body) to influence emotions, and create different forms of understanding. Qualitative market researchers are only just beginning to work with such 'experiential knowing', and to think about such concepts as the 'enactive mind' – a mind that is shaped through many types of interaction with the internal and external environment. Observational research and re-enactment of processes can access insights that cannot be obtained through interviewing, as explained by Philly Desai in Book 3.

Humanistic psychology supports phenomenological and clinical research approaches, and emphasises richness and depth of data rather than statistical evidence, so is of particular interest to qualitative researchers.

---

**Box 3.1  Maslow's Hierarchy of Needs**

Maslow's Hierarchy of Needs is a good example of a Humanistic model, as it integrates a whole raft of personality theories into a dynamic system, which is based on the potential for growth and change.

Maslow saw human beings' needs arranged like a ladder. The most basic needs, at the bottom, were physiological – air, water, food, sex. Then came safety needs – security, stability – followed by psychological, or social needs – for belonging, affiliation, esteem, love and acceptance. At the top of the ladder were the self-actualising needs – the need to fulfil oneself, to become all that one is capable of becoming. Later in life Maslow added cognitive needs – the need to understand, aesthetic needs and transcendence – a need to help others find self-fulfilment. The theory was that basic needs have to be met before higher ones can be achieved, although Maslow acknowledged there were significant exceptions, such as Gandhi. Self-actualisers were people who managed and attained the higher needs.

Maslow's model (often in a restricted form) is widely used in marketing, human resources and organisational development. It is very helpful in explaining the priorities people have, and in predicting where the next level of needs will lie once the basics have been satisfied. However, it is likely that Maslow himself would have been unhappy about some of the marketing uses to which his model is put. He was appalled at the use of LSD in the 1960s to provide 'instant peak experiences' as he felt that the idea of buying a peak experience devalued the whole concept. He would be unlikely to agree that buying expensive clothing labels is a sign of self-actualisation. Nevertheless, given that 'motivations, needs and desires' are the stated territory of qualitative market research, his model is invaluable as a picture of how these may be inter-related.

---

## A Change of Paradigm for Advertising and Qualitative Market Research

The psychoanalytic model used by the early motivational researchers was based on a doctor–patient style of relationship. The patient was passive, lying on the couch, while the analyst decided the true meaning of the patient's symptoms. This reflected an early view of the researcher–consumer relationship – the consumer went through experiences and the researcher tried to analyse them. As Lannon and Cooper write in their article on Humanistic advertising, 'Consumers were considered fairly ignorant of the process, subjects to be dealt with as in a laboratory rather than listened to creatively' (1983: 201). It was assumed consumers knew little about how advertising worked, therefore a whole range of questions was not even asked.

Humanistic psychology emphasises the person as an active agent; choosing what to pay attention to, making meaning and exercising choices and responsibilities. The brand and its advertising is seen as constructed by the consumer, rather than imposed on the consumer. This simple but powerful shift in perspective enabled a new research approach, with questions and techniques that ask how and why the consumer constructs a brand in a certain way; what the meaning is of certain behaviours, what values are communicated by the symbols attached to the organisation, and how these fit with people's own desires for change and development.

The Humanistic perspective assumes that respondents will take a much more active and responsible part in the research process. They are not there to provide material for interpretation by an all-knowing figure (the 'analyst' researcher); they are capable of engaging in a joint process of discovery with the interviewer. Research has become much more 'respondent-centred', the emphasis being on understanding how others construct meaning and the role this plays in their lives.

The view of respondents as individuals embedded in, and influenced by, a social and cultural context has added to the usefulness of the group discussion as a way of understanding these influences as well as individual needs. Furthermore, the model is open to other approaches that discover shared meanings, including observation and experiential techniques.

## But the Concept of the Unconscious Survives ...

The new language and methodology arising from Humanistic psychology might suggest that the unconscious is no longer a relevant concept. However, many Humanistic psychologists subscribe to the psychodynamic view and believe that the processes of growing up and socialisation encourage people to develop barriers and defences against their insecurities, and the 'real self' is left at the core, waiting to be rediscovered. Rather than the unconscious being a Freudian basement full of primal urges, it is the source of authentic being. To become all that a person can be (a definition of self-actualisation), a person has to first discover who he or she really is.

## A BRIEF OVERVIEW OF CULTURAL ANALYSIS AND MINOR THEORIES

Since so much of the work produced by qualitative market researchers is out of the public domain, it is not possible to be definitive about the extent of use of theory in the profession. The literature shows that some researchers do use aspects of psychodynamic and Humanistic theory overtly, and the interest in semiotics and cultural analysis is increasing as it becomes more obvious that consumers cannot tell interviewers everything they need to know. (See Book 3 for a lucid account of semiotics and cultural analysis in relation to qualitative market research.) Chandler and Owen are proponents of a cultural approach; seeing it as re-defining the remit of the qualitative market researcher:

> Our proper object of study is not the individual either as a rational or a psychological being. Our proper object of study is the cultural web of meaning and behaviour which we call 'consumer culture'. (Chandler and Owen 1989)

As Valentine and Evans (1993) point out, qualitative market research itself has a set of codes, of taken-for-granted assumptions. The dominant codes are that 'good research' is required to 'go deeper', and that the deeper responses are more authentic, powerful and valuable than superficial, 'rational' responses. The emergent codes, the new way of thinking, create a completely new frame of reference. In the new frame, the operative distinction is not between 'deep' and 'surface' responses, but between different and equal perceptions of the self, perceived in the imagination, shaped by different linguistic modes of expression and driven by cultural rules of language (1993: 129).

Semiotic analysis can be undertaken without interviewing consumers at all, and indeed there are a number of theories that do not impact in a very overt manner on interviewing. It is important to note, however, that the theoretical mindset will affect what questions are asked, how they are asked, and how the answers are noticed and interpreted. A researcher looking for explanations at the cultural level may spend more time investigating what respondents believe 'People Like Us' do and value. At the social level the researcher may ask the group to comment on their own interactions as a way of clarifying the dynamics involved, whereas a researcher taking a psychodynamic perspective might choose to understand individual dynamics by asking whether 'a part of you' feels a particular way or whether there is some inner conflict.

Spackman, Barker and Nancarrow (2000) note that there has been a shift in marketing from the 'grand, all-encompassing, universal explanations of human behaviour' to 'theories focusing on narrow bands of a culture and sub-culture'. In their view, a series of 'micro-insights' may well be more appropriate 'to inspire, convince and stimulate action' (2000: 95). Sometimes these will be marketing-oriented and may well have been formulated within the client organisation: sometimes these come from the numerous mini-theories in psychology and related disciplines – concepts such as cognitive dissonance, attribution theory, locus of control, mental set, social scripts, change processes and self-efficacy, for example. These theories often provide helpful explanations for a particular set of circumstances. This book does not have the space to describe these in detail, but most introductory texts to psychology should explain them. Hayes (1994) covers them all.

## CONCLUSION

This chapter shows how the prevailing theories have affected the interviewing relationship – the approach to the respondent, beliefs about what research might be able to uncover and interviewing styles. There are two distinct but interconnected trends in the way that theory is affecting the practice of qualitative market research. The first is a re-interpretation of what used to be taken for granted as 'the unconscious', or hidden influences on attitudes and behaviour. The 'hidden' that researchers now aim to uncover includes the adaptations made by the self to fit in with social and cultural expectations, and the cultural assumptions themselves. Researchers also have to deal with the hidden in the sense of neurological processing that takes place out of conscious awareness yet still influences behaviour – a theme expanded on in Chapter 4.

The second trend is making the use of theory more explicit – a necessary undertaking in order to be able to use the new insights in interviewing and analysis.

### KEY POINTS

- The history of qualitative market research has left it with a psychological legacy. It started with the assumptions inherent in the psychoanalytic view that it was both possible and desirable to explore some aspects of the unconscious, and that this information would be useful to research users. Commercial research still aims to go beyond the consciously aware and rational but uses a broader range of theoretical frameworks.
- The Freudian psychoanalytic approach deals with the tripartite structure of the individual psyche, and can be useful, but Freud's emphasis on the psychosexual has limited the acceptability of his theories. The work of other analysts is broader and could be of interest to researchers.
- The concept of the unconscious has become naturalised, become a part of the taken-for-granted assumptions about the psychology of the individual. It is therefore important to explore some of the original theory, and to note that despite a paradigm change to Humanistic psychology, the notion of working with material that is not directly accessible to consciousness has remained as a key identifier of the qualitative approach.
- The ideas of Humanistic psychology changed the assumptions about how the consumer/respondent can make meaning of the world and participate in the research process. Respondents are seen as active interpreters, socially situated and capable of insight into their own behaviour.

- Some psychoanalytic concepts have become more widely disseminated through a psychodynamic theory approach, which bridges psycho-analysis and Humanistic psychology. The key aspects of this are:
  o The psyche is split into different parts.
  o Conflicts arise between them.
  o Interactions between the parts may not be conscious but affect behaviour.
- Social psychology offers theories that formalise the assumptions that researchers make about the value of the interaction between respondents. The broadly ranging Humanistic psychology is the source of many models of interaction and influence, some of which are explicitly used in marketing.
- Qualitative research is increasingly working at an even broader level, with the values, assumptions and meanings integrated into the culture. Researchers' needs to provide useful insights for clients are also encouraging the use of mini-theories from a range of disci-plines, which provide useful explanations for particular sets of circum-stances rather than attempting to account for human behaviour in general.

# Implicit and Explicit Theories that have Influenced the Practice of Qualitative Market Research

The influence of psychoanalysis and Humanistic psychology has been so pervasive that these theories have not only informed expectations about the type of information qualitative market research can uncover, but also have shaped the practice of interviewing. This chapter reveals the legacy of Carl Rogers in particular and describes some of the main concepts involved.

A brief review shows that the principles of group dynamics have become part of the practice of qualitative market research, although some moderators may not be aware of this. Neuro-Linguistic Programming (NLP) describes itself as being about the 'structure of experience' and originated partly from studies of excellence in interviewing. It is a good source of refinements to current practice.

New developments in neuropsychology have major implications for interviewing. Information about the mechanisms of processing and retrieval guides interviewers towards appropriate techniques and challenges some traditional thinking. Finally, there is a review of the assumptions and limitations of the interviewing process; based on the theoretical perspectives that have been discussed.

## IMPLICIT THEORY FROM HUMANISTIC PSYCHOLOGY: CARL ROGERS AND QUALITATIVE MARKET RESEARCH BEST PRACTICE IN INTERVIEWING

Carl Rogers was the most influential American psychotherapist of the twentieth century. He 'humanised psychology and psychotherapy', pioneering a major new approach to therapy, known successively as the 'non-directive,' 'client-centred' and 'person-centred' approach (Dolliver, 1995). Rogers carried out and encouraged an unprecedented amount of scientific research on counselling and therapy, and his work was so influential that he was even published in the *Harvard Business Review* (Rogers and Roethlisberger 1991).

Carl Rogers believed that 'the individual has within himself vast resources for self-understanding, for altering his self-concept, his attitudes and his self-directed behaviour' (Mearns and Thorne 1988). Therefore, the role of the therapist was not to be diagnostic and prescriptive (as in analysis), but to provide the conditions under which the client's inner resources for change and self-understanding could be tapped. The Rogerian method of interviewing (or key elements of it) can be applied to many forms of communication that are not therapy-based. As a result of Rogers' influence, there is an increased respect for the needs and capabilities of the respondent, and an understanding that good interviewing practices can have a beneficial effect on respondents. Respondents may initially attend for the money they receive, but if they are listened to well, they feel their views are valued and respected.

### Conditions of Establishing a Good Interviewing Relationship

Rogers analysed the factors that influenced the interviewing situation and made clear a number of techniques, such as 'active listening' and 'reflecting' that encouraged authentic response. Researchers adapted his concept of non-directive interviewing as a means of minimising possible biases in questioning techniques. Rogers defined three conditions for establishing a therapeutic relationship: these to some extent apply to the interviewing relationship too – **empathy, genuineness and unconditional positive regard**.

> Empathy requires the much more complex and delicate process of stepping into another person's shoes, and seeing the world through his or her eyes without, however, losing touch with one's own reality. (Mearns and Thorne 1988: 26)

**Empathy** is not sympathy or pity. It involves entering the frame of reference of another, and sensing how he or she feels about things as if those feelings were the interviewer's own. The 'as if' is crucial, since it stops the interviewer becoming overwhelmed by the feelings of the other. Empathy is best regarded as a process rather than a technique. It is important that the empathy is accurate, and that it is communicated to the respondent. Some of the benefits of empathic listening are lost if the respondent is unaware of how tuned in the interviewer is. There are various levels of empathic responding, and used incorrectly, respondents can feel they are being categorised and judged. Most qualitative market research aims for two levels of empathy:

- Showing an understanding and acceptance of the feelings and thoughts that have been expressed.
- Showing an understanding of the respondent that is just outside the respondent's immediate awareness, an interpretation, a re-phrasing,

which comes across to the respondent as an insight or a crystallisation of how they were feeling. This interpretation should be checked out with the respondent before being attributed to them.

**Genuineness** is about knowing oneself and reacting to others in an *authentic* way. Rogers felt that most people needed some self-development work themselves before they were capable of being genuine. (This is because as children we have to adapt to others' demands, and in order to protect ourselves we construct a 'false self'. This needs to be dismantled in adulthood to allow the 'true self' to come through.) For the person-centred counsellor this is a life-long journey. For the qualitative market researcher, it is more likely to mean a willingness to drop a professional front or a personal façade. There are times when the best laid plans go wrong, and the interviewer who is able to say, 'help, I'm stuck' or 'I don't know how to ask you this' is likely to achieve a more constructive result than the one who tries to maintain the illusion of professionalism.

**Non-possessive warmth** or **unconditional positive regard:** this creates the trust that enables the building of a relationship, and can be hard when the researcher feels he or she does not like the respondent. An important distinction is made between liking or approval of the behaviour and of the person. Researchers may be working with attitudes and behaviours they don't approve of, but can establish a working relationship on the understanding that the person him or herself is not intrinsically bad. It requires the ability to accept others, and to set aside the common judgemental mistake of identifying people with their behaviour ('he acted in a selfish way, therefore he is a selfish person').

### Rogerian Principles as Best Practice in Interviewing

Rogerian principles of interviewing still dominate thinking on best practice in qualitative research interviewing and moderating. Researchers aim for transparency, realise they have to value their respondents in order to benefit from working with them, and build as much empathy through active listening as they can. It is important to understand that qualitative market researchers do not aim for pure 'non-directive' interviewing. This approach is used in therapy as it challenges the client or the group to take power, and create their own agenda. Non-directed or 'unmoderated groups' (see Chapter 5) are valuable in understanding respondents' agendas, but are vulnerable to disruption by process problems such as dominant respondents.

A high level of interviewer neutrality and non-directiveness is likely to be perceived by the respondents as being distant, disinterested and patronising. Respondents want some guidance on what to talk about, although they do not want to be told what to say. However, qualitative market researchers have retained aspects of the non-directive approach, such as being careful to avoid giving their own opinion, re-directing questions back to the respondents, and trying to avoid being judge-mental. They routinely use open questions and probing, paraphrasing or reflecting what respondents say as a way of clarifying its emotional significance, and trying any way they can of getting below the 'false self' into one of the layers below.

## IMPLICIT THEORY FROM THE STUDY OF GROUP DYNAMICS

The study of group dynamics is the study of social forces that operate on individuals as members of human groups, and looks at the relationship between the individual and the group. As this section will explain, the practice in recruiting and moderating groups has evolved in such a way as to minimise the negative effects of these group processes, while enhancing the positive effects.

Kurt Lewin is widely recognised as the founder of modern social psychology. Much of his work was based on experiments with groups, as well as observation of real life situations. Group dynamics developed quickly as a research topic because it was so useful: from factory workers assembling products in small groups, to gang behaviour, prejudice against minority groups, management decision-making, learning and education and psychotherapeutic groups. For a thorough description of the scope of group dynamics, see Forsyth (1990).

### *Normative Practices in Qualitative Market Research in the UK*

At some point, the concept of a 'standard' group discussion gained accep-tance in the qualitative research community. It aimed to have seven to nine respondents, strangers, relatively homogenous in status. It lasted 1½ to 2 hours, had an introduction, a warm-up and then discussion of the key questions. Despite constant experimentation with all the variables involved – fewer people for longer times, mini groups, conflict groups and numerous other variations – this remains the foundation of 'how things are done'. Most commercial researchers feel these practices work well. Unless they have studied social psychology, they are probably not aware of all the theory underpinning the things they do.

First, a distinction has to be made between process and content or task. The *process* is what happens between people in the group – who has what type of interaction with whom, and why. It can be thought of as an unconscious will of the group, which can get in the way of the content. This is because groups trigger unconscious feelings and associations about previous experiences of authority, needs for emotional space, rivalry with others etc. The task is to answer the client's question through discussion, and this forms the *content* of the group. Content consists of the questions and answers, the verbalisations, the images, the material that is produced by the group. Process is much less visible to the untrained eye, but can be noticed through patterns of communication, through role-playing in the group, through body language and group energy.

The moderator's job is to manage both the task and the process. A moderator who is fixated on the task can end up with a compliant or rebellious group without having any idea why, while a moderator who is too people/process-oriented will have enjoyable and interesting groups, but be unclear whether all the research objectives have been covered properly. Process and content are inter-related, in that respondents use the content to express their feelings about the process, especially in the early stages of the group. For example, respondents who have taken a dislike to each other or are struggling for dominance in the group will not say so overtly, but will take up opposing positions on a research issue. The content is used to send signals about feelings within the group, and moderators need to be able to disentangle the two.

### *The Principles of Group Dynamics*

The 'standard' group discussion format that has evolved, maintains control of many process factors. (The following description of the theory of group dynamics is selective in choosing those aspects most relevant to commercial market research groups.)

Group dynamics defines a group as two or more individuals who influence each other through social interaction. According to Forsyth, most groups have from two to seven members. Size has a direct effect on group dynamics, since the larger the group the more formalised its structure needs to be. Larger groups might also suffer process loss (time and effort expended on activities not directly related to task accomplishments) and social loafing, where effort per person decreases as group size increases. Qualitative market research groups are of a size where the structure can remain informal (and be maintained by one person), and social loafing is minimal. As topic guides become fuller and more detailed, qualitative market researchers have less time to spend on managing the process, which is why some prefer to work with group sizes of six rather than eight.

Chapter 5 discusses some specific reasons why people might enjoy participation in research groups. Group dynamics offers a number of other views on the general benefits of group participation – meaning the many natural groups people belong to, as well as groups set up specifically to achieve an objective (see Box 4.1).

---

### Box 4.1    Benefits of Group Participation

- Groups offer(ed) protection against environmental dangers. Sociobiology suggests natural selection favoured individuals who prefer group living. Humans may be instinctively drawn to other humans

- Group membership satisfies many basic psychological needs: affiliation, power and expression of inclusion, control and affection. Freud suggested that adults in groups (unconsciously) replay their experience of family life

- Discussion in groups allows us to evaluate the accuracy of our personal beliefs and attitudes – social comparison. We seek additional information if we feel ambiguous about something, and we bolster our self-esteem by comparing ourselves with others

- Groups satisfy our interpersonal needs; social support, a buffer against stress and loneliness

- Problem-solving can be more effective in groups

- We are drawn to some groups because of the mechanisms of interpersonal attraction: similarity, complementarity, proximity, exposure, reciprocity and basking in reflected glory – in a prestigious group. Group membership is more rewarding when people discover they like each other

---

Although Box 4.1 shows that people like being in groups with attractive people, they also prefer to avoid unattractive people. There is a tendency to avoid individuals who possess objectionable characteristics, people who are boring and those who are physically unattractive. Research respondents have little choice about their co-members, which poses an additional challenge for moderators, who do not usually cite attractiveness amongst the recruitment criteria.

### Stages of Group Formation and Development

One of the characteristics of groups is that they change over time. For market research groups, the Tuckman model is most appropriate for giving detailed guidance on stages of group formation and the moderator's role at each stage. Tuckman (1965) describes the original model, although various users and commentators have adapted the model for their own purposes. An alternative is Will Shutz's FIRO model (Schutz 1958); while for workshops other models can be seen as more appropriate.

The Tuckman model of stages of group formation can be summed up as follows:

| | |
|---|---|
| **Forming** | Inclusion issues, a 'dependent' group, anxiety |
| **Storming** | Control and power issues in relationships |
| **Norming** | Create norms and trust to work in harmony |
| **Performing** | Cooperative, task-oriented works as a whole |
| **Mourning** or **adjourning** | Signal the end so people can prepare to let go |

The model was not developed specifically for research groups, so the stages in a research group are sometimes not so clearly developed – particularly the storming and norming phases. (This is also because respondents are recruited to avoid the differences in status that often underlie storming.) However, an awareness of these is helpful as they can send warning signs of potentially troublesome respondents. In training, researchers are shown videos of the stages which they can then relate to their own experience. In most cases, a big difference can usually be seen between the body language and energy levels at the start of the group and once the group has 'warmed-up'. Moderators who do not signal the mourning phase well enough (and have run a good group) will find themselves with respondents who are reluctant to go home.

### Forming

Since the group members don't know each other, or the task, they are dependent on the moderator as a leader figure. Leaders are supposed to have a strategy, take care of their followers and exert appropriate discipline and authority. Moderators have to briefly take on this leadership role at the beginning (and be prepared to step into it again if the group gets into difficulties later), but they must also signal that they do not want to hold all the power that comes with the position. One way this is done is by emphasising how valuable and important respondent's views are.

Group members may be feeling any or all of: dependent (in an almost childlike way), ignorant, powerless and in need of affection and approval (from the leader – and the rest of the group). Moderators notice a palpable sense of separateness in the group. The way the interviewer handles the introduction and warm-up needs to address and resolve all of these issues, otherwise the group will stay dependent and say only what the moderator wants to hear, or become resentful and full of difficult respondents.

It is important to explain the task and the circumstances of the group (confidentiality, recording, any viewers and their role) and to give guidance on group behaviour. This is done both verbally by emphasising no right or wrong answers, individual opinions and an equal interest in each person's opinion, as well as non-verbally by the way the moderator behaves. The moderator also has to be careful to establish appropriate patterns of interaction between members of the group at this stage.

### Storming

This phase may not always be very evident in research groups, nor does it always happen after forming – the group can run into storming at any time. It can't happen until respondents have been empowered – or they decide to take power for themselves. Storming is about share of voice, and influence on the group. Signs of storming include challenges to the moderator or other respondents, strong statements of individuality, and physical disruption (like standing up to get drinks or having a cigarette). Sometimes the challenges are concealed in a jovial atmosphere and one or two of the witty comments may have hidden barbs. It is at this stage that the dominant respondents emerge, while others may go into a passive sulk – which is why it is important to deal with potentially difficult respondents early on. Moderators may have to signal or repeat that they need to hear equally from everybody to spread the power evenly through the rest of the group. There needs to be an early acceptance of negative views (sometimes respondents are just testing to see if the moderator really meant any view was alright), combined with a balance of the positive. The energy at this point may feel quite negative.

### Norming

In a sense, this happens right from the start of the group, when the moderator models the group norms during the introduction. It develops rapidly once storming is over and the power issues are sorted. This is when the group seems to take off, and there is some harmony and cooperation. It is a good time for additional explanations about the task and making plans for handling it.

Every group needs 'rules' to keep it safe and functioning well. However, respondents also negotiate these between themselves, often without being aware of it. Some of the more obvious ones are the level of politeness or banter, the degree of disclosure, the turns that people take in speaking. There may also be norms around decision-making in the group, which will emerge as patterns. Some norms will only become known if one is broken. For example, if somebody becomes abusive it will become clear that this is unacceptable to the group, and the group will look to the moderator to openly state that rule. Challenging or explicitly stating norms may feel uncomfortable to do, but it helps keep the group functioning well.

### Performing

There is a sense of concentration, task orientation and flow. Moderators love this stage of the group. This is when it feels easy, everyone communicates well, energy is high, and the moderator feels it has all been worthwhile. Individual disputes are forgotten as the whole group focuses on the task. This is the time to introduce projectives, stimulus material and any difficult questions for the group to work with. One of the ways to move into performing is to introduce a task that will absorb the group as a whole and enable them to forget all their earlier concerns. A task such as product or brand mapping (see Chapter 8), where respondents become involved with the research materials, often speeds up the process. This stage uses group energy, so after a time it runs out, and the group slips back into one of the other stages, or needs to have a quiet period to re-energise.

Although the Tuckman model is often described as a linear model, moderators will recognise that there is some repetition and cycling of the stages. For example, a disagreement during an exercise in the performing stage may set off some storming again, after which the group settles down with a new spirit of cooperation (norming) and comes back to performing later.

### Mourning or Adjourning

Having gone through all of these stages, the group will have bonded to the stage where it feels more comfortable to be in it than to be separate from it. The mourning stage is to enable group members to let go. It should be signalled when approaching the last topic or in the last ten or so minutes, that the group will finish soon. It is good to ask respondents if there is anything they want to say that they have not been able to say so far – it really 'closes the circle'. Mourning has a relaxed but satisfied energy about it.

The Tuckman model is not the only model of group development. There is also Will Shutz's FIRO Model (Fundamental Interpersonal Relationship Orientation), which is based on his theory that there are three fundamental dimensions in interpersonal relationships – inclusion, control and openness. Inclusion parallels Forming and Norming, Control parallels Storming (and Norming to some extent) and Openness relates to Performing, so these map into the Tuckman model quite well.

Experienced moderators use their sense of the group energy as a guide to what may be happening and what they should do about it.

> You can walk in and tell the mood of a room with your eyes closed, you can tell by feeling that energy; there is an aura, if you will. I've had to learn a long time ago when to turn on energy – perform – and when to pull back energy, and to turn it off when you are done. Because when you leave a group you are on a high. (Moderator interview)

| Stage | Underlying Processes | What you notice/ what happens | Moderator's task |
|---|---|---|---|
| **Forming** | People feel separate, dependent, anxious, relatively powerless<br><br>Who am I here? How will I fit in?<br><br>What are the risks? | Awkwardness<br>Caution<br>Light social chit-chat<br>Testing behaviours | Empower and make safe by explaining the task, modelling behaviour, and encouraging interaction<br><br>Behave as you would want them to |
| **Storming** | Share of voice, demanding attention<br><br>Challenges to moderator and others<br><br>'Pecking order'<br><br>Opting out or rebelling | Challenge moderator or each other; play up<br>Question the task<br>Emphasise individuality<br>Dominant and passive emerge<br>Physical disruption | Signal strongly that you value all opinions equally<br><br>Accept negative views but look for the positive too<br><br>Stop potentially dominant respondents becoming overbearing<br><br>Look for fight or flight responses |
| **Norming** | Sense of harmony, cohesion and support<br><br>Norms emerge<br><br>Group takes off | People take turns in speaking without you having to ask<br>The energy feels more positive and harmonious | Notice and reinforce norms<br><br>Deal with any implicit rule-breaking<br><br>A good time to make plans and set agendas<br><br>Keep channels of communication flexible |
| **Performing** | Individuals are subservient to the group<br><br>Roles are flexible and task-oriented | Sense of concentration and flow<br>Everything seems easy<br>High energy<br>Group works without being asked | The time to introduce difficult issues, stimulus material or projectives |
| Re-adjustment: Performing uses energy, so after a while the group slips back into one of the other stages before it can perform again | | | |
| **Mourning or Adjourning** | Completion of the task and disbanding of the group<br><br>May be a sense of loss and anxiety<br><br>Need for closure | If you haven't completed it, people may not want to go<br>If someone leaves early, the process feels incomplete | Signal that the end is coming<br><br>Summarise to give a sense of achievement<br><br>Ask if there is anything else they want to say<br><br>Thank them |

FIGURE 4.1 *The Tuckman model of the group life cycle* (adapted by Joanna Chrzanowska)

Moderators can sense whether a group feels safe or not, when there are unspoken issues developing, or when something is not being said. It may be that they are responding to subliminal cues from respondents. There is a developing theory of 'group energetics' propounded in the UK by William Bloom,[1] and it may be that this will give further insights into managing group processes on an intuitive and energy level. It is not possible to evaluate how valid the theory is, but it is a valuable notion to use.

There is also a group socialisation theory, which points out that group membership is a two-way process. Individuals are changed by belonging to a group (assimilation), and groups adjust to their members (accommodation). Moreland and Levine (cited in Forsyth, 1990) theorise that there are three reciprocal socialisation processes (evaluation, commitment and role transition), which operate at each of five stages (investigation, socialisation, maintenance, resocialisation and remembrance). While the two-way process idea is of interest, this model is unnecessarily complex for qualitative market researchers to use.

Similarly Bion's Basic Assumption Approach (which was developed mainly for psychoanalytic groups) and covers such concepts as dependency, fight–flight groups and pairing groups, goes too deep into the dynamics for most short-term research groups. (See Gordon and Langmaid, 1988 for a discussion.)

### Power in Groups

Power or social influence is defined as the capacity to influence others, even when they try to resist this influence. The patterns of power distribution in the research situation are many and varied. Moderators can be in a situation where they hold too much power (for example, working with children) or too little – as when a young female interviewer has to interact with a senior businessman. Interviewers use body language, other non-verbal signals and verbal techniques to manage the power relations and generally prefer to avoid imbalances if possible.

Group dynamics researchers have identified a number of specific tactics that can be utilised to gain power and influence over others. These include: promises, rewards, threats, punishment, expertise, discussion, requests and demands, instruction, persuasion, negotiation, group pressure, persistence, *faits accomplis*, manipulation, supplication, ingratiation, evasion and disengagement.

Of these, discussion, negotiation and group pressure make regular appearances in qualitative market research groups, as do requests from the moderator. Moderators are likely to use *faits accomplis* when time is short – for example, stating that some aspects of a product or service are not open to discussion or change. Respondents are prone to use expertise, ingratiation, evasion and disengagement in their challenges for power, resulting in the traditional 'difficult respondent' roles of dominant, soapboxers, passive and quiet respondents. The specific skills for dealing with these will be discussed in Chapter 7, but the key is for the moderator to avoid coercive influence tactics. This is because coercive tactics often lead to submissive, passive reactions. They generate outward compliance rather than internalised attitude change, and are linked to a number of dysfunctional group processes.

## Implications for Group Moderators

Given a choice, people prefer to associate with those who do not outperform them in areas that are very relevant to their self-esteem. This factor is controlled to some extent in qualitative market research recruitment procedures, which aim for a degree of homogeneity. Researchers particularly avoid mixing workers and their supervisors, health care professionals at different levels of status and knowledge, and any other situations where a person might feel internally judged by another member of the group. When working with children or teenagers the age bands are kept very narrow, so that they are all at approximately the same level of development.

**Interpersonal behaviour** in groups is determined by role, status/power, attraction and communication. Some of the research on leadership is relevant to moderators, as is some of the work on decision-making processes.

*Roles* create stable patterns of behaviour in groups, but can be stressful when they are not clearly defined (role ambiguity) or call for incompatible behaviours. Gordon and Robson (1982) and Cordwell and Gabbott (1999) showed that respondents found a non-directive approach to interviewing stressful. (Moderators were being so neutral that respondents didn't understand what was expected of them.) This approach is not part of their expectation of a group leader or group manager role, so there is role ambiguity.

Part of the moderator's task is to observe and manage the roles; delegating some of the task roles and ensuring that respondents aren't stuck in socioemotional roles such as jester or devil's advocate. Client viewers often comment that some respondents seem to be 'leading', without understanding that all groups naturally develop temporary leaders. The danger is when the leadership becomes overly influential, coercive, or excludes others.

Some people compete with each other for *status* in groups. Researchers notice this as respondents subtly compete to mention they have a desirable car, the most fashionable perfume, or go to the gym the most. Group dynamics shows people also compete in process terms. For example, individuals who speak rapidly without hesitating, advise others what to do, and confirm others' statements are often more influential than individuals who display cues that signal submissiveness. The role of the moderator is quite literally to moderate the effects of these plays for status; stopping the 'dominant' respondent from having too much space and encouraging the quieter (more submissive) ones to speak by showing how their contribution is valued.

Much of the group dynamicists' research on *leadership* is less relevant to qualitative market research, as moderators try to avoid strong leadership. Moderators need leadership behaviours that improve interpersonal relations within the group, and task behaviours that help the group complete its tasks. Moderators aim to avoid leading the group in terms of the findings.

Qualitative market research groups often do not take decisions in the same way as task-focused work groups. Respondents are encouraged to provide as much information and insight as possible, but the group itself rarely takes a decision about what to do (unless the moderator uses this as a technique to clarify opinion, for example the 'all things considered' question as suggested by Krueger 1998).

*Groupthink* (Janis 1972, in Forsyth 1990) is when groups make decisions that individual members know to be poor. Moderators can sense a version of this when there is some discomfort in a group about the conclusions that have been reached. Groupthink is more likely to occur when group members feel they have to be nice to each other, are not challenged on any unrealistic views and are pressured into making choices before they are ready. In qualitative market research, groupthink is avoided by impartial moderating, use of sub-groups to discuss issues and validation of individual views.

Qualitative market researchers are encouraged to give equal weight to opinions within the group, and may even temporarily support a minority view in order to provide some balance. When summarising, the moderator includes the range of views that has been obtained, which largely avoids the *polarisation effect*. (A group decision can be more extreme than the mean of its individuals, because there is pressure from the majority to make the minority conform.) Balanced moderating also helps to avoid the *conformity effect*, which was so dramatically demonstrated by Asch in the 1950s. The experimenter's confederates estimated the lengths of various lines as much longer than they visibly were. A third of the experimental subjects agreed with these estimates, rejecting the evidence of their own eyes in order to conform to the group. (A repetition of the study by Perrin and Spencer in 1980 found fewer people actually lied, but their anxiety levels were just as high.)

## THEORIES ABOUT PROCESS THAT ARE USED EXPLICITLY

Rogerian principles of interviewing are transmitted through researcher apprenticeship and training. Researchers learn how to listen well and ask good questions but may not be told from where the principles derive. However, the following theories, Transactional Analysis, Personal Construct Psychology (PCP), Neuro-Linguistic Programming (NLP) and neurological theories about information processing are not embedded in research processes, and therefore have to be learnt about and used explicitly.

### Transactional Analysis

Eric Berne, who developed Transactional Analysis, was originally trained as a Freudian analyst and wanted to develop a theory combining the psychoanalytic tripartite view of the psyche with Humanistic principles of personal growth and change. Qualitative market researchers will recognise some of the ego states as ones they need, or meet, in the course of their interviewing.

Eric Berne made complex interpersonal transactions understandable when he recognised that the human personality is made up of three **ego states**, each of which is an entire system of thought, feeling and behaviour from which people interact with each other. The distinctions of Parent, Adult and Child ego states form the foundation of Transactional Analysis theory. These states have distinct and observable behaviours, and moderators may need people to be in different states at different stages of the group. The moderator who models these states consciously at the start of the group will find a much more cooperative and flexible response emerges when required later.

- The **Parent** is based on memories of our parents' thoughts, feelings and behaviours. It is engaged on any occasion when people need to be responsible, reassuring, nurturing, protecting and directing. The other side of the Nurturing Parent is the critical, judgemental side, even punishing – the Controlling Parent.
- The **Adult** state is objective, rational, evaluating and appraising. It is all about working out options and using decision-making capabilities. The downside of this state is that it can be too detached and computer-like.
- When a person is in **Child**, they are consciously or unconsciously replaying child-like behaviours, thoughts and feelings. The Natural or Free Child state is: spontaneous, playful, creative, physical and expressive of emotions, full of joy and life. But the child is also guilty and shamed, and *adapts* to the needs of parents by developing strategies such as being cute or sulky, being a goody-goody or a rebel.

**Transactions** refer to the communication exchanges between people, but can cover communications between people and brands or organisations. Adult-to-Adult, Parent-to-Parent and Child-to-Child transactions are complementary, as are most Parent-to-Child. The aware moderator will know someone in the Child ego state will often bring out the Parent in others, while Parent-to-Adult transactions are often difficult. This model can explain some of the strange or uncomfortable dynamics that can take place in a group, as well as some of the reactions consumers have towards communications with brands and organisations.

Berne observed that people need *strokes*, the recognition every person needs to survive and thrive. Socially dysfunctional behavioural patterns he called *games*, the repetitive, non-productive transactions to obtain strokes that reinforce negative feelings and self-concepts. Examples are 'Why Don't You?', 'Yes But', and 'I'm Only Trying to Help You'. There are specific research versions of games, such as 'I Never Watch Advertising', 'I Know Somebody Else You should Aim this At' (see Gordon and Langmaid 1988).

Judith Wardle's shows in Book 6 how Transactional Analysis relates to advertising communication research.

### Personal Construct Psychology (PCP)

This merits a brief mention in this section because it provides very powerful ways of understanding individuals' mental maps of their world (or in PCP jargon, construct systems.) It is very much a theory of the individual and the techniques are hard to use in groups, although several companies have found statistical ways of aggregating individual results to define commonalities.

Personal Construct Psychology was founded by George Kelly, who wanted to find a way of understanding how individuals 'construe' (make meaning of) the world. One of the main premises is that we all see the world through our own lenses, which are fashioned from previous experience. His theory has been described as 'every man his own scientist'. Each person notices repeated themes in his or her life, names and categorises them, and applies these labels to the people and situations they meet. PCP makes no value-judgements about the validity or logic of these constructs, and sees them as part of an overall construct system. Construct hierarchies have a pyramidal structure, with lots of detail at the bottom, while the higher levels are more general and inclusive – and more important to the person's sense of identity.

The interviewing process called laddering moves up the pyramid, from very basic distinctions about the world, to very meaningful distinctions. For example, starting with some descriptors of coffee, such as 'strong', and asking 'why is this important to you?' at each level of the hierarchy, can rapidly end up dealing with a person's core constructs – their sense of identity. It is a repetitive technique and can be intrusive, so it has to be used with great sensitivity.

In PCP, 'constructs' are applied to 'elements'. They can be people or roles, situations or products, types of packaging etc. The Kelly Grid uses comparisons between elements to elicit the constructs, and then requires some form of rating of each element. The grid then shows the patterns of interaction between them, rather like a cluster analysis.

### Neuro-Linguistic Programming (NLP)

Qualitative market researchers have been able to learn a lot about interviewing from Neuro-Linguistic Programming. NLP was developed by Richard Bandler and John Grinder, who studied those they regarded as excellent communicators and therapists such as Fritz Perls and Milton Erickson. They also studied the work of linguists Alfred Korzybski and Noam Chomsky, using the skills they learnt from the early work to facilitate the study of others. They wanted to analyse excellence in such a way that it could be taught to others.

NLP is a generative process – so it is always changing and growing. It is described as being about *'the structure of experience'* – how people take in and process information. In this respect it is content-free, as summed up by Korzybski's well-known saying

It is the map, not the territory.

Reconceptualised by Richard Bandler as

It is the menu, not the meal.[2]

Somewhat like qualitative research, NLP has blended theories from other disciplines.

- **Neuro:** Neurological system – the way senses translate experience into thought processes, both conscious and unconscious. It relates to the physiology as well as the mind. Mind and body are seen as one system.
- **Linguistic:** The way people use language to make sense of experience, and the way it is communicated to others. Language patterns reflect who people are and how they think.
- **Programming:** Is the coding of experience. Sequences of behaviour and thinking patterns that result in 'experience'. Awareness of these sequences enables people to code the structure of their own and other people's experience.

Apart from its use as a communication model, its analysis of 'logical levels' and the model of perceptual positions which make good analytical tools, NLP offers specific pointers on questioning skills, rapport building, state management and dealing with different sensory modalities. A good outline introduction to NLP is *Principles of NLP*, by O'Connor and McDermott (1996).

### Questioning and Listening Skills

NLP emphasises the precise use of language. 'Trying' to achieve something includes the possibility of failure. In research, asking what people *think* of an idea is vastly different to asking what they *feel* about it, although the two are sometimes used interchangeably in conversation. External events are subjected to our internal filters before they are stored. Researchers can learn what filters a person is using by listening carefully to their language – what do they generalise, distort, leave out and presuppose? Chapter 6 gives some examples of how NLP can improve and refine questioning.

These events are stored as internal representations, which have visual, auditory and kinaesthetic (feeling) components. NLP provides the tools to access these, which enable a closer examination of the overall experience. NLP can work with memories or concepts, and provides a means of exploring stimulus material in depth. An NLP approach can enable respondents to actually recreate past experiences in the research rather than just describe them.

### Rapport-Building

Rapport-building skills are clearly of major interest to interviewers, both in dealing with respondents and with clients. NLP treats rapport as an on-going process with many different levels. It is based on the notion that people who are similar feel more comfortable with each other. NLP teaches skills to increase and decrease the perception of similarity. Some of these are non-verbal and include matching and mirroring of body postures, gestures and even physiological characteristics, such as rate of breathing.

There is also a verbal component in mirroring and matching respondents' primary 'representational systems'. Bandler and Grinder noticed that some people used visual language a great deal ('it appears to me', 'do you see what I mean?', ' it looks clear') while others use auditory ('I'm tuned in', 'I hear you', 'loud and clear') and others use kinaesthetic language ('I need to get in touch with', 'get a grip', 'it was a blow'). They hypothesised that this might be related to a preference for processing experiences in one represen-tational system than another. While the evidence for this is mixed, an inter-viewer who is able to notice and respond to the use of a particular system is able to build rapport faster than somebody who just uses body language.

Some people do work within a predominant system, and it is important to be able to recognise and work with this. Asking a kinaesthetic respon-dent to 'picture the scene' is to set them a hard a task and create a mental barrier – they don't picture scenes. Alternatively, asking them to 'imagine what it feels like to be there' taps straight into their way of thinking and experiencing the world.

### Noticing and Using States

NLP posits that these internal representations of experiences elicit emo-tional states, and claims that through development of sensory acuity to very minor physiological indicators, such as facial muscle tension, skin tone, breathing rate and position, an interviewer can be aware of what state a respondent is in and when that state changes. This enables the interviewer to ask better timed and more appropriate questions.

NLP also has tools for working with one's own state. The Emotional Intelligence competence of being able to motivate oneself does not have to be a happy accident. In a process called anchoring, desired states are evoked from memory, are re-experienced as fully as possible with all the senses, and the resulting internal state is 'anchored' using a small gesture or a visual trigger. If this is done powerfully enough, triggering the anchor brings the feelings of the desired state back into consciousness.

## Neuropsychology

NLP developed in part from neurological theories of the brain, and these are increasingly impacting on both qualitative and quantitative methodologies. Understanding how stimuli are processed and stored in memory explains many observable research phenomena. Respondents arrive at a group wondering how they can possibly spend 2 hours discussing a subject like toothpaste or food colouring. They are amazed to discover that they 'know' (remember, think, feel and intuit) a great deal more than they give themselves credit for, and that they could probably talk for hours. Whether the concept of the psychoanalytic unconscious is accepted or not, it is becoming clear that the majority of information received by the brain is processed out of conscious awareness. Parts of the brain function semi-autonomously and emotional tone can be added to stimuli during processing. The categorisation and storage of the clusters of associations we conceptualise as knowledge is both complex and fluid, and memory research has important implications and challenges for interviewing.

### The Triune Brain

Paul MacLean is credited with the theory that human evolution has left us with a legacy of three parts to the brain (Greenfield 2000). They are all interconnected and function seamlessly, but have different roles and characteristics, and process information in different ways. The three evolutionarily distinct parts have evolved from the bottom up; the higher centres are elaborations of lower and more ancient parts.

- The primal **'reptilian'** brain at the top of the brain stem and spinal cord. (It is called reptilian because humans share this with alligators and lizards.) This part constantly monitors the internal and external environment, controls basic physiological needs, and may be thought of as the source of our basic instincts.
- The emotional **mammalian** brain (limbic system structures). This evolved to provide more sophisticated systems of noting and reacting to stimuli, as well as parenting and social bonding behaviour, which is

needed when there are dependent young. The structures are involved in both emotion and long-term memory.

- The higher thinking functions of the **human** neocortex (cerebral cortex). This is a large layer covering the more primitive structures – and is responsible for higher faculties such as calculation, language, music, religious experience etc.

The parallels with Freud's Id, Ego and Superego, as described in Chapter 3, are notable, if not exact.

> The bottom line was that the brain stem was the source of the driving power, the energy that underscored everything we did. In this sense MacLean's view of the function of the brain stem was akin to Sigmund Freud's *Id* – the provenance of blind, brute urges to copulate and attack, to create and destroy. (Greenfield 2000: 3)

A more appropriate comparison is with Maslow's Hierarchy of Needs, which states that basic physiological needs have to be met before higher order ones become important. The reptilian brain deals with physiological needs, the mammalian brain with safety, the need to belong and basic forms of self-esteem (enough to be able to fit into the hierarchies of social structures) while the human neocortex deals with the need to understand, aesthetic needs and higher ideals such as self-actualisation.

Occasionally a 'decision' about behaviour can be made without reference to the higher structures at all – what might be called 'an instinctive response'. This is a built-in safety feature that would have been very useful for hunter–gatherers. In his book *Emotional Intelligence* (1996) Daniel Goleman calls this an 'emotional hijacking' and points out that it is often a very inappropriate reaction for modern living, triggering outbursts of hostility, anger and fear in circumstances that are rarely life-threatening.

Of more relevance to researchers is the role of the 'mammalian' brain in attaching an emotional charge or 'flavour' to the stimulus. It is important to note that in this context 'emotion' does not describe a conscious feeling, although it may be later modified in the higher cortex to create a more subtle form of emotion. These emotions are indeed a vital part of decision-making. People who are cut off from this emotional centre through some form of brain damage live in a world of grey neutrality. They have no real reasons for avoiding anything or choosing to do something else. They can't even decide what colour jumper to put on in the morning, let alone find the motivation to go to work, cook dinner or play golf.

### Brain Hemisphere Specialisation

Another theory that has had significant influence is that of brain hemisphere specialisation, more colloquially referred to as 'left brain, right brain'. The theory is that the left half of the brain emphasises language, logic, linear processes and sequences in time, while the right half of the brain emphasises forms and patterns, images and pictures, imagination and emotion, and is holistic and time-free in its processing. This is an exaggeration, since the two halves work closely together and are linked through the corpus callosum – a neural bridge. However, there are physical differences between the two halves of the brain and 'almost every mental function you can think of is fully or partly lateralised' (Carter 2000).

For most qualitative market researchers the significance of the theory is conceptual. It has created an understanding that they are trying to access 'right brain' material (emotions, concepts, images) through 'left brain' methodology – since interviewing is primarily language-based. This has clarified the usage and value of non-verbal tasks, and why analytical forms of questioning can give misleading results in certain cases. As early as 1981 the advertising agency Young and Rubicam released a paper called 'A Brain Hemisphere Orientation Towards Concept Testing' (Hecker), which contained the key thought that 'left brain concepts should not be tested with right brain concepts because respondents will probably select the former' (1981: 55). Other variations on this theme have since appeared and resulted in awareness that it is important to create the right conditions for evaluation of research materials. This is a particularly important issue for advertising research where a verbal deconstruction of an idea can destroy its intended emotional impact.

### Pre-Conscious and Out of Awareness Information Processing

In 1981, Norman Dixon's book *Preconscious Processing* suggested that:

- Stimuli can be registered in the brain without conscious awareness of them
- These stimuli can be subjected to semantic analysis as a form of screening
- Some non-conscious stimuli can have observable physiological effects
- Such stimuli can change the conscious emotional feelings of the individual.

The psychoanalytical assumption that many decisions are influenced by factors outside of consciousness can be seen in a new light, as neuro-psychological research reveals that a great deal of information is screened by the brain and processed out of conscious awareness.

> Only one millionth of what our eyes see, our ears hear, and our other senses inform us about, appears in consciousness. Metaphorically, consciousness is like a spotlight that emphasises the face of one actor dramatically, while all the persons, props, and sets on the vast stage are lost in the deepest darkness. (Trinker 1998)

The mind has a tremendous amount of data streaming into it from the senses every second. The eyes alone scan two billion bits of data per second. Our consciousness relies on automatic recognition of objects and situations because this frees our conscious mind up for other things. This recognition is not formed on the basis of an objective reality – but what the mind has been trained, and expects to see. Past experience influences what is perceived and attended to.

Whereas pre-conscious processing may not be stored in memory, Robert Heath suggests there is a similar sort of automatic out-of-awareness processing that does store information in memory. This type of information processing is described by Heath (1999) as 'low involvement processing'. Three aspects of this are significant:

- We cannot stop ourselves from doing it. It is an automatic process that continues even when we think we are not paying any attention.
- The data that is scanned and stored is not subject to very much processing because low involvement processing does not use much working memory.
- However, it can be considered a simple form of learning, since various parts of the data are connected to each other and to simple concepts through association. The more often we see something, a pack, an ad, a logo, the stronger the connections become.

In contrast, high involvement processing is what most people would call thinking and analysis – a conscious process of cognitive evaluation. Because this process takes up so much of the human attention span, it would be impossible to process the multiplicity of advertising and brand messages received everyday using it. Heath concludes 'that nowadays we tend to process virtually all advertising using low involvement' (Heath 1999: 148).

In relation to advertising and brands, Heath suggests that the associations formed by repetitive low involvement processing can eventually outweigh those formed through the few occasions of processing by High Involvement. If the research project is to assess advertising, then to show people the ad and ask them questions about it is a high involvement process, and will reveal different things from a technique designed to visually or verbally unravel the associations people have with a product or a brand. Heath also mentions that if the associations are linked to simple 'somatic markers' (the emotions or effects attached by the mammalian brain) they can exert 'powerful influence on intuitive decision-making' (Heath 2001).

Swindells (2000) talks about 'the invisible mechanics of consumption', putting forward the theory that consumers are more likely to be 'doers' than 'thinkers' when it comes to decision-making, suggesting that the associations created through low involvement processing (here called residual advertising images) may affect product choice. Consumers do not have the time or the interest to think through all the minor purchasing decisions they make, so it may be that their attitudes to a product only consciously crystallise once they have bought it and used it.

> Residual advertising images are frequently activated by behavioural choice situations and followed at some time in the future by attitude change – the brand is then evaluated in the process of consumption. (2000: 45)

This implies that if qualitative market researchers set out to examine the decision-making process with the assumption that all the cognitive processing happens before purchase, they may be missing some very important insights.

Apart from stream of consciousness interviewing (see Memory below), the main techniques researchers have that would help to uncover the associations formed by low involvement processing come within the range of so-called projective and enabling techniques, described in Chapter 8. Those who are proponents of these find them useful and insightful, but are rarely able to explain exactly what they are uncovering with them. The theory of low involvement processing starts to address exactly what is meant by the 'intuitive' and offers a potential route into the further understanding and development of such techniques.

### Non-Conscious Information Processing – the Implications for Interviewing

If information is processed and stored unconsciously then respondents will not be able to recall directly what they have seen and experienced. Interviewers need a bank of techniques that can access the way the brain works, and need to rely on cues rather than unprompted recall. Various types of association techniques use relevant cues from one part of an associative network to bring to consciousness the other links that form part of that network. Word association is the most basic, but can be augmented by mind mapping (literally displaying the network visually) and also product and brand mapping. These techniques are covered in Chapter 8. Laddering, described briefly under Personal Construct Psychology, is a way of making explicit the hierarchical structures in networks of memory and meaning.

The ultimate cue is to be in the context where the stimulus and behaviour takes place; or to recreate that context as far as possible. This involves getting respondents out of living rooms and studios and working in more natural settings. Visual techniques such as creative visualisation and collages are another way of accessing stored information that the person may not be conscious of, particularly information that has an emotional effect attached. Respondents can pick out pictures they intuitively like and associate with a brand, but may not initially know why.

### The Nature and Limitations of Memory and How These Affect Interviewing

Parkin (1999) describes long-term memory as having three components – procedural (remembering how to do things), episodic (episodes and events in personal history) and semantic (facts and knowledge about the world, meanings of words, and the linguistic rules for manipulating them).

Alan Swindells (2000) uses the distinction between semantic and episodic memory to suggest that interviewers need different techniques for accessing each. He claims that episodic memory can only be captured by Individual Perceptual Focus Interviews, to capture the 'stream of consciousness' nature of current reactions to a stimulus through interior monologue. Whereas, 'semantic processing is likely to be the outcome of a group discussion or an individual depth interview' (2000: 47). Therefore, for any project in which it is important to capture the nuances and idiosyncrasies of consumer impressions, the best methodology is one where consumers report their experiences as directly and immediately as possible.

Parkin (1999) comments that some psychologists have found it hard to show that these two types of memory represent separate systems. This is because facts are learnt (semantic) during the process of experiencing things (episodic). Nevertheless, there may be great value in taking a more overtly experiential and individual approach: asking consumers simply to react, think aloud, at the time of interacting with the stimulus, minimally processing what they say.

Another significant discovery about the storage of memories is that they are not stored as entire individual experiences, but as schemata or scripts – models of the world based on experience, that can be used as a basis for remembering events. Memories are reconstructed rather than retrieved. Memories are encoded selectively. The more emotionally significant parts, those that fit with what people already know or expect, and the more meaningful, take priority over what has been judged insignificant or immaterial.

Even so-called 'flashbulb' memory can be unreliable, and reconstructions of memories change over time, with subsequent retellings, as the schemata are slightly altered each time they are used. This is more of a problem for the police, who have to rely on eyewitness accounts of events, and who have developed a 'cognitive interview' to improve recall. (This involves mentally reinstating the external environment, the internal environment – feelings – and recounting the event in a variety of orders and from a variety of perspectives.) These 'multiple retrieval paths' are also of use to researchers who may need to get an accurate memory of an incident.

Other memory effects have implications for qualitative researchers.

- **Context**, or **state-dependent** learning, where the memory is best retrieved when the person is in the same physical or emotional state as when the memory was laid down. Not many important memories will have been created in research viewing studios!
- **Cued recall** – although the cue helps to bring back the memory, it may also be integrated into the memory itself.
- **Mood congruence** – people in a good mood will tend to remember more positive experiences, while those who are depressed will focus on the negative.

| Effect | Description | Implications |
| --- | --- | --- |
| Episodic memory | Episodes and events in personal history | Best captured by individual personal focus interviews to capture the stream of consciousness nature of the event, before it is processed into semantic memory – as it would be in groups |
| Primacy and recency | People remember things at the beginning and the end better | Worth bearing in mind where recall tasks are important – product features, or information communications |
| Context-dependent memory | The environment in which the learning takes place can be built into the memory | Get out more |
| Cued recall | Cues bring the memory to mind but may affect it too | Neutral and accurate cues are best |
| Mood congruency | The mood people are in at the time will affect what type of memories they bring to mind | Get your respondents into the appropriate mood for dealing with a subject |
| Misinformation effect | The questions asked can influence perceptions and recall | Be very careful! Avoid dramatic language |
| Memory distortions and mindset | People's memories are influenced by the recent past | Structure topic guides to avoid creating strong mindsets – or break them at appropriate points |
| Implicit memory | People are affected by memories they are not aware of | Consider whether there is a way they might have been 'primed' beforehand |
| Associated and disassociated memories | Seeing the memory through your own eyes or seeing yourself from outside as an observer | Use the appropriate method of recall for accessing or distancing from emotions |
| Cognitive interview | Use multiple retrieval paths to improve accuracy of recall | Where accuracy is important don't be afraid to ask for a variety of descriptions |

FIGURE 4.2   *Summary: memory effects and their implications for qualitative research*

- There is **confirmation bias**, in which people see what they expect to see, regardless of whether it happened or not.
- It has also been shown that the **method of elicitation** can affect the memory itself. In a famous experiment, people were shown a film of a car crash, and then asked questions about it. Some were asked how fast the cars were going when they 'hit' each other, others how fast they were going when they 'smashed into' each other. The latter form of questioning got higher estimates of speed, as well as other details such as broken glass – there wasn't any. Furthermore, the higher the perceived status of the interviewer, the more sensitive people were to suggestions made by the style of questioning.
- Like mood, **mindset** affects retrieval of memories. People will more easily retrieve memories relevant to the recent past – for example, things they have just been discussing, than on a subject that has just been introduced.
- **Implicit memory** – recent experiments have suggested that people can be affected by memories without being aware of them. Several studies have shown that preferences and feelings can be shaped by specific encounters people do not remember explicitly. For example, negative words flashed up too quickly for conscious perception later caused people to feel hostility to a fictional person. People who glanced through magazines briefly later claimed to prefer the products featured in that magazine – without having any awareness they had seen them in the magazine earlier. (Schacter 1996)
- In retrieving a memory, it is possible to be either **associated** (you are seeing the memory through your own eyes) or **disassociated** (seeing the memory from the outside as an observer.) More significantly, an associated perspective is more likely to bring up an emotional component to the memory, while the disassociated perspective reduces the emotions associated with the memory.

## A REVIEW OF THE ASSUMPTIONS AND LIMITATIONS OF INTERVIEWING WITHIN THE THEORY OF QUALITATIVE MARKET RESEARCH

### Difficulties with 'Hidden' Material

Qualitative market research has accepted the concept of the unconscious, a concept which by definition can only be inferred and not known directly. Although it has good explanatory value in some situations, there are cognitive psychologists who believe it should have the status of a temporary working hypothesis only until the workings of the brain are fully understood.

Qualitative market researchers' propensity to borrow parts of theories and adapt them for commercial use ignores the context in which the theories were developed in the first place, which was usually one of healing, personal development, or a change process. However, researchers do not aim to change their respondents and it has to be questioned whether this is an appropriate usage of the theoretical material.

Although neuropsychological research seems to provide evidence that non-verbal approaches can elicit important information not normally available to consciousness, this research itself has to be treated as provisional and subject to change. The temporary influence of Wilder Penfield's experiments with 'holographic' memory was based on dubious evidence and psychologists' selective perception.

If the new memory research is more accurate, then there are several questions about what is actually being accessed when interviewers ask people to describe a process or situation from everyday life. It seems likely they are remembering a general schema and filling in the details, and they might alter these details according to their expectations, their mood, or the style of questioning of the interviewer. Furthermore, they will store this new version, and alter it yet again the next time the story is told.

Respondents are often not in the same physiological state as they were when engaging in the behaviour, which means that valuable cues and aspects of experience are lost.

### The Social Situation of the Interview

Respondents do literally construct themselves, that is, they tell stories of how they think they are and how they think they behave – but these might not be confirmed by observation. There are occasions when the 'truth' does not matter – it is argued that what counts is the perception of the situation, since this will influence behaviour. However this verbalised perception of the situation may be a post-rationalisation for behaviour that was generated by low involvement processing – an out-of-consciousness, largely non-verbal process.

Secondly, he or she is 'doing an interview' – in a specific social situation, that might aim to be like natural conversation but isn't. No matter how well phrased the interviewer's questions and probes, the respondent cannot feel he or she is having a normal conversation. The interviewer asks all the questions and holds the agenda. Should the respondent unwittingly break this rule and ask a question back, it is likely to be avoided and turned back. The normal rules of conversational turn-taking will be changed, there will be an imbalance in the amount of speech between the two, more chance of monologues, and the respondent will be aware that he or she is speaking in what Conversation Analysis would call a non-formal institutional setting (Hutchby and Wooffitt 1998). The difference becomes clear once the tape recorder is switched off and the respondent seems to relax into a more casual mode – often asking the interviewer the questions they have held back.

Being aware of the interview as a social situation also means that the respondents will be presenting themselves in what they imagine is a favourable light. Erving Goffman's *The Presentation of Self in Everyday Life* (1971) talks about 'performance', conceptualising any kind of social inter-action as being 'on stage'. Many of the routine activities of life which researchers are interested in are off-stage preparations for the 'social front', yet ironically the interview itself is an 'onstage' situation. Can the interviewer ever really see the respondent 'off-stage'? This issue is magnified in the group situation where respondents are trying to make a good impression on each other as well as the moderator.

### The Limitations of Language

Since interviews are predominantly language-based, deficiencies or biases in the use of language will lead to biases in the findings. Much is made of the interviewer's apparent neutrality in the interviewing situa-tion itself, but the interviewer will have a background that has absorbed cultural assumptions about male and female roles in society, about how ethnic minority groups and homosexuals should be treated – not to men-tion expectations of how people should behave in their everyday lives. The respondent's account will be filtered through all these lenses. One example is feminism.

Since the 1960s, feminist authors have continually raised issues about how male-dominated power structures are, how 'public' language reflects male concerns and issues more than female ones, and how women them-selves collude in what the feminists describe as oppression. Even if the interviewer has some awareness of the issues, the ways of thinking are so deeply ingrained that it is very difficult to completely step outside the patriarchal framework. There is a beautiful example in a woman describ-ing the relationship with her analyst:

> [He] was obviously a kind man, he never told me what to do, what to think, or laid interpretations on me ... The oppression lay in who he was, the questions he didn't ask, and the material I didn't present. It lay in the way I felt when I arrived at his house on a bicycle and he drew up in his large car; the sense I had that he must see his wife and family as normal and my household as a sign of my abnormality. To be cured would be to be capa-ble of living like him. (Ernst and Goodison quoted in Rowan 1983: 140)

Marjorie De Vault writes that 'the lack of fit between women's lives and the words available for talking about experience present real difficulties for ordinary women's self-expression in their everyday lives' (1990: 97). She argues that women 'translate' into another set of linguistic terms when they describe their experiences, and as a result, parts of their experi-ence are lost. She suggests that when women say 'you know', put in hesitations, search for appropriate expressions, that these are signs that language is lacking the words for a full description of that experience.

Devault highlights this in the context of a feminist approach, but the problem is not unique to women. Any interviewer who has tried to get men to talk in detail about their romantic relationships will come up against similar problems. Aspects of life that are not commonly discussed tend to have underdeveloped vocabularies. Socioeconomic group and educational level is another factor that affects respondents' ability to explain themselves. Indeed there is a complex relationship between class, gender and power, whereby a well-educated woman might have a far greater facility with language (formal and informal) than an uneducated man.

### Hidden Assumptions

Interviewers will not only have cultural assumptions and biases, but also ones implicit to the work itself, such as how they view the consumer. Without being aware of the literature, these assumptions may influence their approach. Valentine and Gordon (2000) review various models of the consumer that have been used by qualitative market researchers. These include: the marginalised consumer, the statistical consumer, the secretive consumer, the sophisticated consumer, the satellite consumer and the multi-headed consumer. They then go on to reconstruct the twenty-first-century consumer as 'a "subject" that continually constructs identities for itself by entering into the process of consumption' (2000: 84). Each model of the consumer implies a different kind of research approach, yet many researchers are not clear which model they subscribe to, or might change the model according to the situation.

Nevertheless, despite the criticisms and potential drawbacks, interviewing remains the key methodology used in qualitative market research. The lesson is to bear in mind the limitations and assumptions of interviewing techniques, and to take steps to minimise the disadvantages, such as:

- finding and using alternative, non-verbal methods of expression, both to access information more purely as it is stored in the brain, and to help consumers describe their experiences;
- using bracketing, a process in which interviewers identify their biases and bracket them – set them aside temporarily, to enable them to see and hear respondents more clearly;
- obtaining information on an individual basis as well as in groups;
- becoming aware of the cultural codes and symbols implicit in each topic they are studying so they can see outside the taken-for-granted framework;
- using non-interviewing methods to triangulate – to compare the learnings from interviewing against other views of 'reality'.

## CONCLUSION

Many qualitative market researchers do not realise the extent to which their craft skills are based on theoretical principles. The work of Carl Rogers has left researchers with a set of sound principles for interviewing skills, while the theory of group dynamics is integrated into common practice in running groups. Researchers who have learnt the craft can work very effectively without knowledge of either of these, but are often helped in their development by an appreciation of the roots of what they do.

Researchers are constantly challenged to work more effectively, not only by the changing requirements of clients but also by new developments in NLP and neuropsychology, which show that interviewing techniques and processes need to be constantly reviewed and updated.

### KEY POINTS

- Theories about what can be discovered through research have been influenced by psychoanalysis, but qualitative market researchers have rejected the psychoanalytic paradigm for the interviewing process, as it can lead to unfounded interpretations. Instead, interviewers have taken the spirit of Carl Rogers – and some of his techniques – to develop an approach that is more respondent-centred and less subject to interviewer bias.
- The theory of group dynamics shows that current practice in setting up and moderating groups has evolved to minimise negative forces in groups and build on the positive forms of interaction. A model of the stages of group development provides a basis for understanding why moderators use different approaches and techniques at different stages of the group.
- Group dynamics also draws attention to the issue of power and social influence in groups, and ways of managing it.
- Transactional Analysis is a theory of personality and communication based on the Freudian tripartite model of the psyche, but without the psychoanalytic baggage. Personal Construct Psychology gives insights into how each person 'construes' their own view of the world and is the source of the Kelly Grid technique and laddering.
- NLP fine-tunes questioning and listening skills, increases the effectiveness of rapport-building and helps interviewers manage their psychological 'states' and those of their respondents. It also helps make more effective use of some types of stimulus material.
- Some of the emerging theories about brain function and memory can be used explicitly by researchers to examine, explain and develop further the skills and techniques of interviewing.

- Although it is the most widely used method in qualitative market research, the assumptions and limitations of interviewing have to be acknowledged. These include:

  o  researchers' propensity to borrow selectively from theories;
  o  difficulties with 'hidden' material;
  o  the provisional status of some of the neurological research;
  o  the limitations of language;
  o  hidden assumptions;
  o  the selective and reconstructive processes of memory;
  o  the social situation of the interview.

- Although these limitations lead to a more realistic view of the nature of the interview, they do not undermine the value of the process itself, especially since good interviewers take account of many of these factors.

## NOTES

1  Details of his educational programme can be found at www.holisticpartnerships.com
2  This is from an NLP training course.

# The Interviewing Relationship

This chapter delves into the foundation of qualitative interviewing – the interviewer–respondent relationship. The role of the interviewer/ moderator is critical to the quality of the output, as the interviewer is the research instrument. The chapter discusses the factors involved in the development of good interviewing skills. Looking at how respondents experience the process gives further insight into best practice in interviewing, and specific problems in interviewing and moderating are discussed. This chapter examines in turn: the interviewer, the respondent, the nature of the relationship, the effects of viewing facilities on that relationship, and what can go wrong.

## THE INTERVIEWER/MODERATOR AS THE RESEARCH INSTRUMENT

It is a repeated theme of commentators that the quality of the interviewer makes a difference to the quality of the research output.

> ... Much more is vested in the skill and expertise of the individual researcher than is the case in other more structured forms of research ... (MRS R&D Sub-Committee 1979: 113)

> Only a few researchers will have the sensitivity to group processes that will make them eligible to conduct group interviews since social scientists are not routinely 'trained' in interviewing in their graduate school experience. (Frey and Fontana 1993: 33)

Defining 'quality' in any objective sense has proved to be elusive, perhaps because of the 'horses for courses' nature of qualitative market research, where the key is choosing the appropriate researcher for a project and establishing a good working relationship. The Market Research Society R&D Sub-Committee recognised the difficulty of establishing a yardstick for quality, using the analogy of falling in love – '.... you'll recognise that feeling – and the more satisfying depth of understanding – is there' (1979: 111–12).

The concept of interviewer as the research instrument is broadly accepted in many forms of qualitative research. In the context of writing about the 'long (cultural) interview' McCracken (1988) comments that it is a useful metaphor because 'it emphasises that the investigator cannot fulfil qualitative research objectives without using a broad range of his or her own experience, imagination, and intellect in ways that are various and unpredictable' (1988: 18).

## THE DEVELOPMENT OF INTERVIEWING AND MODERATING SKILLS

### The Role of Training and Experience

Cowley (2000) has proposed a taxonomy of skills for strategic qualitative market researchers, in which the core operational skills in groups are only one level out of seven. This is an important reminder that interviewing is just a part of being a qualitative researcher; there are also intellectual and problem-solving skills, background frames of reference, operational skills to do with setting up, analysing, reporting and presenting, not to mention people, project management and sales skills. His research, based on interviews with Australian qualitative market researchers, indicates it takes time to develop these skills and competences.

According to Cowley, from induction to two years was normally a 'learn the techniques' stage with watching, practice and mentoring. If people had not made it after two years then they would not. From three years to about eight years there was a long, hard, development of skills, and towards the end of this a desire to have highly stimulating projects to work on, or a 'burn out' (2000: 30).

In the UK, the main industry bodies, the Market Research Society and the Association for Qualitative Research, have regular programmes of courses. Independent training is also available, while some of the larger companies organise their own training and development programmes. The learning from these courses has to be integrated through the practice of interviewing. Moderators watch each other work, occasionally co-moderating. Many moderators analyse their own tapes, giving further opportunities for learning about process as well as content.

Learning to drive makes a good comparison. A novice driver has to learn the codes and regulations of using the roads, and to coordinate the basic skills of driving a car. Inexperienced interviewers find it difficult to be listening actively and constructing new and relevant questions at the same time. The hours of practice turn conscious incompetence into unconscious competence, freeing up internal resources to be fluid, sensitive and creative. Experienced interviewers are better at getting from A to B, realise more quickly they ought to be at C, are better able to find the scenic route, and can avoid traffic blockages.

The QRCA (Qualitative Research Consultants Association) website in the USA offers '25 Reasons to Use a Professional Qualitative Researcher'. It emphasises researchers' skills in fluidly dealing with the unexpected, creating a safe climate, being able to probe effectively, dealing with sensitive topics and pulling out hidden meanings, dealing with difficult respondents and defensive behaviour, sorting out anomalies and psychological issues to provide more insightful and relevant research. This is aimed at discouraging amateurs who want to try it because it looks so easy.

### Emotional Intelligence and Personal Qualities

The MRS R&D Sub-Committee produced a view that 'the best researchers have a wide and often disparate range of personal abilities and qualities':

> They must have intellectual ability yet show common sense and be down to earth! They must show imagination, yet be logical. While an eye for detail is essential they must have conceptual ability. They must become involved yet remain detached. They must show 'instant' empathy, yet project themselves neutrally. They must be able to identify the typical, yet think beyond stereotypes. They must be articulate but also good listeners. (1979: 114)

Daniel Goleman (1996) has synthesised a great deal of psychological research into the concept of emotional intelligence or EQ (Emotional Quotient), which can be applied in business. His description of EQ competences (see Box 5.1) could have been tailor-made for researchers.

---

### Box 5.1   The Main EQ Competences

- **Self-awareness:** How well do we know our own emotions? Do we understand where our emotional responses come from?

- **Self-regulation:** How much do we allow our judgements and behaviour to be influenced by our feelings? How much do we allow ourselves to use our intuition?

- **Motivating oneself:** What is it that drives us? How do we deal with obstacles and setbacks?

- **Empathy:** Recognising emotions in others. How well do we read the feelings of others? How do we read a group's emotional currents and power relationships?

- **Handling relationships**: How well do we manage the emotions of others?

- **How well do we listen?** How do we nurture relationships, deal with conflicts, manage change, work as part of a team, and negotiate with others?

(Goleman 1996: *passim*)

---

Dealing with difficult respondents (and clients) requires the ability to know and manage one's emotions. Other aspects of EQ include dealing with the unexpected in a research study; understanding how emotions might affect judgements and interpretation; uncovering 'shoulds' and 'oughts' and self-limiting beliefs.

Interviewers need to be able to trust their intuition, and feel safe in the unknown territory of dealing with others' emotions. They need to be able to access their inner resources when required and know how to create the conditions for success. They have to manage their own energy and that of the respondents. They need to demonstrate congruence in what they say and what they do, and have enough self-awareness to work with difference and ambiguity. Many researchers would describe themselves as being a 'people person' – they are describing emotional intelligence.

### Interviewer/Moderator Variability and Style

Interviewer effect or variability has been extensively written about in the context of quantitative research. In a review of the problem, Collins (1980) highlights the need for good training, particularly on skill in probing and obtaining information in depth (albeit in the context of a quantitative questionnaire). In a qualitative research situation there is much more scope for interviewer effect. The basic sources of interviewer bias clearly acknowledged in the social sciences (Powney and Watts 1987) are:

- **Background characteristics** of the interviewer: age, level of education, socioeconomic status, race, sex and religion – some of which may be (wrongly) imputed by the respondents.
- **Psychological factors** such as the perceptions, attitudes, expectations and motives of the interviewer. Interviewers may unwittingly convey their expectations – both positive and negative.
- **Behavioural factors**, such as the way in which questions are framed and addressed, the amount of time spent on various subjects, the amount of energy and interest shown by the interviewer etc.

Gordon and Robson (1982), warn that

> Even skilled Interviewers convey more than they perhaps wish, by body language, that is ,non-verbal cues. The problems this can create – respondent resentment, distrust, posturing – are greater than those created by Interviewers' misuse of verbal communication. (p. 461)

It is not possible to eliminate these sources, but good interviewers do as much as they can to become aware of them, to manage them in the interviewing situation and to be aware when they are analysing the findings. Strategies that help manage bias include:

- Setting up the interview in such a way that power variations between interviewer and respondent are tempered and controlled.
- Explicitly presenting the interviewer as being there to learn from the respondents and stating a wish to be non-judgemental ('There are no right or wrong answers').
- Creating the interview relationship using behavioural modelling, rapport and empathy. Modelling is used non-verbally to show congruence with the verbal assurances, while rapport and empathy minimise distrust through a constant awareness of the respondent's emotional state.
- Developing respect for interviewees, regardless of personality and background; and setting aside preconceptions and prejudices.
- Having a genuine curiosity about others which motivates when interviewing threatens to become tedious.
- Becoming a skilled listener, aware of their own blocks to listening.
- Having multiple strategies for drawing out people and dealing with 'difficult' people.
- Becoming self-aware of their own communication style, hot buttons and personal triggers.

An early view of the best model for an interviewer was a 'neutral sponge'– somebody whose presence does not affect the others, and who can soak up the information that is given out. It soon was acknowledged that this is unrealistic and that the interviewer has to use his or her personality – while being aware of the possible effects it might have. Recent training methods encourage interviewers to develop their own style, and do what is comfortable for them. In this way, they become a model of naturalness and authenticity for the respondents, who can then feel comfortable themselves. Properly managed, researcher personality and 'bias' is to be welcomed as a way of bringing different insights into a piece of work.

> Given the dynamic and inductive way [qualitative research] operates, it is true that replicability is impossible to prove theoretically. Indeed, I wouldn't want to, since regarding the researcher as a valuable bias in the whole process, I prefer to believe that while the base data may be replicable from one study to another, the interpretation (and consequent action) may differ. (Robson 1989: 8)

## Roles Interviewers and Moderators Play

Interviewers and moderators have to contend with the effects of characteristics that are a consequence of their personality and background, but also choose to adopt a variety of roles that help them deal with the wide range of respondents and situations they encounter. These roles can be temporary, or maintained throughout most of the interview, and can include the following.

- **The deliberately naïve** – very useful where the interviewer truly knows little about the subject matter or fears he/she has a biased view of it.
- **The experienced veteran** – by suggestion rather than demonstration – for dealing with people who have specialist knowledge or skills and would be offended or impatient to be confronted with someone who knew too little.
- **The friend/colleague/peer** – where the researcher has the appropriate social characteristics to fit this role credibly without having also to give their opinions on the subject.
- **The independent 'reporter'** – who makes it clear he or she is having to write a view of the positives and negatives after the research and appears to stay a little bit distant; a handy strategy where the researcher may be the focus of disapproval or anger at a product or a policy.
- **The joker** – to enliven a 2 hour discussion on a low involvement issue like processed peas.
- **The counsellor** – a soft and caring tone for enabling sensitive subjects.
- **The fisherman** – who sets out tasty morsels as bait and waits to see what will come to the surface.
- **The directive taskmaster** – more often a temporary position, but can be applied quite consistently, for example with an unruly bunch of 10-year-olds.
- **The devil's advocate** – for groups where a more challenging perspective is needed to cut through the posturing or temporarily support a product or concept to make sure it gets a fair assessment.

The roles have to be used with sensitivity and subtlety. If respondents perceive the moderator as playing an inauthentic role, this gives implicit permission for everyone else to play roles too. Researcher training emphasises the need to maintain an authentic personal core discernible through these roles to avoid this effect.

## THE RESPONDENT'S EXPERIENCE OF THE RESEARCH PROCESS

### Recruitment

The first contact the respondent usually has with the research process is via the recruiter. (Recruiters are trained interviewers who are paid to gather a specific sample of respondents, often using a recruitment questionnaire, also known as a screener.) They invite respondents to the research location, which may be their home, a hotel, or a viewing facility. In the USA, respondent databases are built up by research agencies and viewing facilities, and the actual recruitment is likely to be done by telephone.

An early study of respondents' experience of attending groups was done by Wendy Gordon and Sue Robson in 1982, and pointed out the vital role of the recruiter in overcoming the mixed feelings many respondents had when invited to attend qualitative research. To achieve a commitment to attend, the recruiter had to overcome distrust by being persuasive and reassuring: by being seen as friendly, open and honest.

The incentive (a cash payment) was very or fairly important for the majority in making the decision to attend, although they also found the experience overall to be enjoyable and informative.

## The Respondent's Experience of the Group or Interview

Gordon and Robson found there was initially some self-consciousness and nervousness about the first interview experience; repeat attendees were more comfortable and relaxed.

Respondents were described as being 'acutely sensitive' to the interviewer during the introductory phase, because they were seeking the 'real' reason for the interview, as well as clues about how they should behave and what sorts of answer might be required. The interviewer was expected to conform to a particular stereotype and anybody who deviated from this had to work harder to win respondents' trust. If the nature of the research and confidentiality issues were not explained well enough, some respondents held back and did not participate fully in the discussion.

During the discussion, respondents variously experienced anxiety about meeting the standards of the group and the moderator, but most were able to say exactly what they thought 'all the time'. Some noted a low level of annoyance at other group members who were too loud or too quiet. They were, however, restrained in expressing this annoyance, which Gordon and Robson suggest is a facet of the 'hidden contract' – a set of obligations which the respondent adheres to as a result of accepting the invitation and the payment.

After initial tensions, most respondents found the experience enjoyable and felt at ease. When asked what the moderator might be feeling, they seemed to understand the moderating task and the interviewer's concern with getting good contributions from everybody – however, they also picked up what may have been impatience, irritation and boredom emanating from some moderators.

A more recent study (Cordwell and Gabbott 1999) confirmed the importance of both the recruiter and the incentive; that the first group attended was more stressful; that respondents might be silent out of anger or frustration with another group member; and that 'experienced' respondents (those who have attended more than one group or interview) had a very clear idea about the role of the moderator. They quote a respondent who had been in a group where a dominant person was not well controlled:

You [the market researcher] should have nipped it in the bud before one person took over. You should have brought everyone else forward, because that is what you are being paid for; everyone's opinion, not just one. (Cordwell and Gabbott 1999: 229)

Respondents valued friendliness, approachability, good listening and encouraging in the moderator, but were also sensitive to a 'snobby' or 'patronising' manner. They also noticed when the moderator was leading towards a particular conclusion, especially if they did not agree with it.

Some moderators are aware they do not manage the group process as well as they might. Researchers attending training courses often bring up the issue of 'difficult respondents' as one they would like to work on. Moderators name several different types that either disrupt the group or do not contribute appropriately. They know what to do in theory, but are concerned about being seen as rude or manipulative if they use any but the most subtle techniques. These researchers are not aware of the extent to which the group members desire control of the 'difficult' elements in their midst.

There does not seem to be any equivalent research on respondents' experience of the depth interview, other than a mention by Gordon and Robson (1982) that individual interviews are 'more stressful' for respondents. In a depth, the respondent has full responsibility for answering all the questions, and the personal dynamic between interviewer and respondent comes into stronger relief. Occasionally the interviewer can be put at a disadvantage and encounter subtle resistance, for example when interviewing recipients of welfare on behalf of the government. There may be a personality clash (which would be moderated by the presence of others in a group situation).

Part of the problem is that the definition of 'depth interview' in qualitative market research is almost infinitely varied. It can range from a short, semi-structured interview to a long, unstructured interview. Sometimes depths are allocated to juniors as part of their training process – with the implication that they are easier than groups. However, an hour-long, open-ended depth is probably more of a challenge for interviewing skills than the equivalent length of group discussion.

Sociological research on respondents' experience of the interview, reported in McCracken (1988), points out that respondents find themselves in the presence of the perfect conversational partner, who listens eagerly to everything they say, makes them the centre of attention, allows them to state cases that may otherwise be unheard, allows them to engage in some self-scrutiny, and even to experience a kind of catharsis. This applies in some qualitative market research, certainly in studies when enough time is allowed for respondents to express themselves. In the majority of research projects, however, the benefits to the respondent are more partial, as the interviewer is likely to discourage excessive attention to topics that do not come within the scope of the study. Nevertheless, they do feel valued. As one respondent said after a group in Leeds: 'My husband would never believe that somebody would pay me to come out and talk!'

### Respondent Issues

How often respondents should attend research groups or interviews is a matter of great debate in the industry, with many moderators holding the view that experienced respondents (those who have attended one or more groups) are easier to work with and more productive than 'virgin respondents'. Virgins, however, can give a fresher and more honest response. Hayward and Rose (1990) studied this issue in detail, concluding that there was no evidence for a *substantial* difference in content related to respondent experience, although the moderator's beliefs about this might well have an effect on his/her perceptions of the group. They also suggested that there was an *experience saturation point,* beyond which respondent experience becomes counter-productive.

An allied issue is the deliberate overuse of respondents by recruiters, sometimes with instructions to pretend that they fit a particular recruitment criterion – a risky strategy, since in-depth probing usually shows up anomalies. Many moderators have had an experience of deliberate cheating in recruitment, although it is impossible to estimate how widespread it actually is. When cheating, or simple misrecruitment, occurs moderators are faced with a decision about whether to expel the person from the group (potentially very damaging to the group) or carry on and make the best of it.

Even if respondents have not taken part in any research before, they tend to arrive with a model of what a research interview is about. They may not know the details, but they see it as a specific situation in which they 'do an interview,' as opposed to having an ordinary conversation. On the positive side, the 'hidden contract' between interviewer and respondent can help the interviewer because 'this ensures among respondents a degree of compliance and willingness to fulfil their part of the bargain'. (Gordon and Robson 1982). One of the surprise benefits is the degree to which respondents will help out inept interviewers by providing detailed answers without prompting, untangling confused questions ('which part of that do you want me to answer first?'), and offering theories about motivation and behaviour without being asked.

The Market Research Society Code of Conduct is very clear that researchers have an obligation to protect respondents' emotional well-being, but interviewers can find themselves in a difficult situation where an interview unexpectedly hits upon a subject a respondent finds distressing. Respondents are free to leave the interview at any time but this is an unsatisfactory and incomplete resolution; and it feels better to calm the emotion and achieve some sort of closure in the situation if this is possible. Where a sensitive subject is being researched, interviewers can prepare back-up information, such as contact details of relevant organisations, which can be given after the interview has ended.

A few techniques such as emotional laddering (see Personal Construct Psychology in Chapter 4) ask very intrusive and potentially upsetting questions. ('Why is it important to you that you should not die in a car crash?' was one question in a recent motoring study.) Some respondents appear to be entirely unaffected, but interviewers have to be especially vigilant in cases like this and decide where to draw the boundaries.

## ESTABLISHING A GOOD RELATIONSHIP

### Using the Awareness of the Process to Deal Sensitively with Content

Research into the respondent experience in groups and interviews has emphasised how acutely sensitive they are to the interviewer at the beginning, and Chapter 4 gives some theoretical perspectives about why this period is so critical.

Briefly, the moderator's introduction and the earliest stages of group formation are the best window of opportunity for dealing with potential problems before they arise, and setting up permissions to deal with other problems if and when they occur. The introduction forms part of both an explicit and an implicit contract with the respondent. It is explicit about the time the research will take, the overall subject, the purpose of the research and the way in which the information will be used. (Some points of information may be held back if it is felt they may prejudice responses, and it is good practice to make this clear: 'You may be wondering what company the research is for. If you don't mind I would rather tell you at the end, because we are aiming for a fair review of all the companies involved in this market.') Collaboration with respondents can be emphasized, and the boundaries of the research situation are clarified.

It helps if the interviewer is as transparent as possible about the nature of the research, is clear about anonymity, the use to which any recordings will be put and the role of any observers. These last can be re-framed from possibly 'critical and judgemental' clients, to people who have come along because the results of the research will make a real difference to their work, and who will value honest and individual opinions.

The moderator needs to indicate that he or she is there to learn from respondents' experience and reactions, and engage people in a problem-solving process by emphasising how valuable their views are. Conformity effects can be drastically reduced if the moderator states overtly that disagreement is very likely and that he or she wishes to hear from everybody equally. The moderator thus gives him or herself permission to control dominant respondents and encourage the quiet ones in one fell swoop.

Not only should the non-verbal signals be congruent with these messages, but also the moderator can reduce anxiety by modelling acceptable behaviour in the group. A degree of seriousness, some jokes where appropriate, even a negotiation of the language to be used: 'Since we are talking about constipation this evening, would you prefer we referred to stools and faeces, or shall we talk about poo and shit?' This saves about 20 minutes while everybody is wondering if they will seem too crude if they say poo, in the meantime having to talk about 'it'. Sensitive subjects are not the only ones that benefit; it helps to establish quickly that the research is about 'nibbly things' rather than the 'super premium snacks' the client thinks they are producing.

## Dealing with the Balance of Power in the Relationship

French and Raven's classic analysis of power bases (1959, in Forsyth, 1990) emphasises five sources of power (see Box 5.2).

---

### Box 5.2   Five Sources of Power

- **Legitimate power** stems from an authority's legitimate right to require and demand compliance. It is often linked to reward and coercive power, and a variant is positional power, where a person's position in the organisation or society gives them power

- **Reward power** is the ability to mediate the distribution of positive or negative reinforcers. This power base is strongest when the rewards are valued, the group members depend on the powerholder for the resource and the powerholder's promises seem credible

- **Coercive power** is the capacity to dispense punishments to those who do not comply with requests or demands

- **Referent power** is based on group members' identification with, attraction to, or respect for, the powerholder. Charismatic leaders generally possess both legitimate and referent power

- **Expert power** derives from group members' assumption that the powerholder possesses superior knowledge, skills and abilities

---

The relationship will almost certainly start with an uneven balance of power – but who has it, and what type of power it is will very much depend on the situation and the people involved. In business-to-business research, and in some medical research, the respondents may be high status individuals to whom participating in research is a low priority, verging on a nuisance. These individuals have powerful positions in their own organisations and they carry that power into the interview setting, sometimes presenting an intimidating façade. They have positional power, which is a variant of legitimate power, and carries across boundaries from the work setting to the interview setting. Although the interviewer has some referent and knowledge power, since he or she sets the agenda for the interview, this may not be strong enough to compensate.

Particularly confusing power issues arise when researching employees of the client organisation, as the researcher has the implicit backing of legitimate organisational power. Despite all assurances to the contrary, taking part in the research may be seen as creating vulnerabilities to reward power or coercive power.

In much consumer research, the researcher is likely to hold the power initially. As convenor, a moderator automatically has some positional power and reward power. Respondents are disadvantaged because they don't know the terms of reference of the research, what they will be asked, or how they are expected to behave. The moderator's power is enhanced when respondents are younger, less well educated and less knowledgeable about the subject.

Moderators can quickly empower the group, through sharing of the research objectives and a transparent way of working, or retain some of the power, revealing information to respondents on a need-to-know basis. There is an argument that the whole situation is an exploitative imbalance of power, since moderators expect respondents to reveal a great deal about themselves without revealing anything in return. The little research that has been done on respondents' experience of the process does not support this argument, suggesting they are more likely to feel empowered, as they feel their views have been valued.

Respondents who do feel powerless will resort to using roles, defence mechanisms and impression management to hide their lack of power. However transparent and empowering the moderator is at the start of the group, there will come times in the group when the moderator needs to assert his or her power in order to control the group. The balance of power is therefore fluid and constantly changing. Most moderators intuitively avoid using what little coercive power they might have as it creates outward compliance but destroys genuine cooperation. They might use referent or factional power, for example breaking up any sub-groups that might distort the findings, by giving tasks to different combinations of individuals.

There are a number of ways in which moderators set up and alter the balance of power, and these are described in more detail in Chapters 6 and 7. Briefly, they include:

- Structural details such as seating position and control of timing and environment.

- Questioning styles and tones of voice which signal assertiveness or warmth and informality.
- The extent to which the purpose of the research is shared with respondents.
- The extent to which the researcher is willing and able to take control, especially when difficult situations arise.

### The Nature of the Relationship with the Respondent

The overall framework is set out within the Market Research Society Code of Conduct and Research Guidelines (and similar codes published by other industry bodies: see Book 1 for more information). This includes protecting the anonymity of respondents, obtaining parental consent for interviews with people under 16, informing respondents of the nature of the research and the purposes for which it will be used, and of any viewing or recording activity, ensuring respondents' emotional well-being is protected, and informing respondents that they need not answer all the questions, and are free to leave before the end.

This is the overt contract – but there is also the 'hidden contract'. By agreeing to take part in the interview, and accepting the money, most respondents feel themselves under a minor social obligation to take an active part in the research. Respondents have been observed helping moderators to frame questions and suggesting additional topics for discussion.

However, the nature of the relationships will depend mostly on the personality and beliefs of the interviewer, and the nature of the topic. Some moderators are more extrovert and outgoing than others, and will end up with 'juicy' groups and interviews. They believe that laughter is a great social lubricant and put energy into making the group lively – although the amount of relevant information content is often no greater than that from a quieter group.

Other moderators may be naturally quieter personalities and/or believe quite seriously in being as non-directive as possible. They are more likely to end up with more serious and relatively quiet groups. In training courses where two or three researchers moderate the same group, the differences in group energy are palpable, but the content appears unaffected.

There are also different beliefs about the extent to which respondents should be involved in sharing the overall objectives of the project. The key benefit of doing so is that they are more motivated, they take some of the responsibility for a good outcome and that often the extra effort gives more insightful findings.

The main drawback is that respondents can forget they are most helpful when in their respondent role; they can start making marketing or advertising strategy suggestions – which is not information that is needed. The discussion or interview is often a learning experience, so attitudes may change because of information acquired during the process.

Some information is therefore held back if it would inhibit a 'natural response'. There are other models for working with respondents, such as Citizens' Juries (for discussion of this see Book 3).

### Other Ways of Building the Relationship

Some interviewers believe in modelling disclosure at the beginning of the interview. They will say something personal about themselves, to encourage the respondent to reciprocate. While this works well, it is good advice to limit this disclosure to topics that are well away from the subject of the research.

Moderators naturally match their own characteristics to the types of respondents. The baseline for an ordinary consumer group would be casual dress, a friendly and interested approach, and a light tone, with some well-rehearsed jokes at the beginning. A business group might require a slightly more formal style, senior citizens a quieter and more respectful style, and so on. In a peer relationship, there is an element of implied mutual understanding. If the age difference is too great, moderators might adopt elements of other forms of relationship, such as older sister or grandson. Moderators sometimes unconsciously take on accents or expressions from the different parts of the country they work in; and they might find themselves speeding up in New York but slowing down in the Southern USA. A Londoner spending three days interviewing in Yorkshire will often return with noticeably flattened vowels!

Moderators who are naturally fluid and move around have an advantage in some groups. It is easier for them to build rapport with individuals, to reflect and change the group energy using their body language, and to include or exclude respondents as might be required.

The moderator–respondent relationship is slightly more of a business transaction in the USA, and in some parts of Europe, due to the nature of the recruitment process. Recruitment companies build up large databases of consumers willing to take part in research for a fee. Consumers give their personal details and wait to be contacted when a suitable research project comes up. Not knowing what the subject will be, the fee is the main initial motivation for signing up. In the UK, it is common practice to recruit respondents as and when they are needed, so they feel they have been specially asked for views on a particular topic. While they are also offered a fee, it is within the context of a particular piece of research.

In a good relationship, the moderator usually feels good about the interview and feels that his or her work has been appreciated.

> When they come to me at the end of a session and they shake my hand and say, 'Hey, I had a great time, thank you very much ...' and I feel really good that they have really opened up and told me what was on their minds, as opposed to 'I'm here for the 50 dollars.' (Moderator interview)

## PROBLEMS OF POOR INTERVIEWING AND MODERATING

Yelland and Varty (1997) examined a number of issues in moderating, questioning the very role of the moderator itself. Their findings about inadequate moderating reflected some of the concerns raised in earlier papers, and the following in particular:

- They pointed to respondents' discomfort with non-directive interviewing, or with moderators who were too carefully neutral and detached. 'Respondents complained at being unable to understand the line of questioning, and unable to voice meaningful opinions in a contextual vacuum' (1997: 92).
- They claimed poorly applied projective techniques, where the purpose was unexplained and the technique rushed, raised anxiety, and could 'have the negative consequence of interrupting the productive flow and prompting ill-considered response'. (Some researchers learn to do the techniques as if they were 'games', without any awareness of the principles on which they work and how they should be handled.)
- They stated that rushing through stimulus material had a similarly counter-productive effect, especially if the material was abstract.
- Yelland and Varty also reinforced the warning that moderators' non-verbal signals cannot be eliminated. Since these signals can indicate approbation or dismissal, they can cause a degree of manipulation by allowing respondents to achieve their general aim of winning moderator approval.
- In addition they found examples of poorly worded questions, ambiguous interventions and confusing use of marketing language (generally the sort of mistakes made by less experienced moderators), and pointed out that respondents experienced the pace of the groups as too fast.

This last is a very important point, as topic guides appear to be getting fuller all the time, which means the moderator has to rush through some sections. Respondents lack time to adequately assimilate concepts, or to understand what is being required of them, or to develop and clarify their thinking.

Yelland and Varty compared 'unmoderated groups' (where the topic and the agenda is clearly explained but the moderator then leaves the room) and groups run by a moderator. The experiment revealed that unmoderated groups are more helpful in understanding how consumers prioritise issues, and in discovering what they see as essential rather than merely desirable. They are more about the consumer agenda than the marketing agenda.

> Unmoderated groups appear more effective in revealing the True Voice of the Consumer (in terms of language usage, communication models, hierarchy of importance and emotional response) ... (1997: 93)

However, the unmoderated groups became very distorted by process issues such as failing to allow for individual dissent and taking a long time to establish a level of cohesion. 'They are clearly less productive in the context of task focus', and 'fail to answer satisfactorily the set of objectives' (1997: 95). Their research confirmed that the moderator has an 'almost indispensable role in prompting discussion of new ideas and introducing new concepts which would not otherwise be considered by respondents' (1997: 96).

The problems mentioned above are caused by a number of factors:

- Lack of training or experience
- Simple human fallibility
- An increasing perception of qualitative market research amongst some clients as a commodity.

The research is squeezed on time and budget; topic guides are overloaded with questions from different departments, moderators are left with little or no time for exploration of new issues, and client participation in the research process can slide into client control of both process and content issues.

In these cases it is not surprising that some consumers are finding the experience less than enjoyable and that moderators have to overlook the needs of the process in order to get through the content. At the same time, however, there is an increasing awareness that there are different and better approaches to be explored, and that a change in orientation will have to happen for researchers to keep up the new demands of an advanced marketing environment (Gordon 1997; Spackman, Barker and Nancarrow 2000).

## THE USE AND EFFECTS OF VIEWING FACILITIES

One of the signs of growing client involvement in the research process is increasing demand amongst clients to attend the groups or depth interviews. The client viewing rooms at facilities can usually seat up to ten clients (and in the USA some are prepared for 20), while client attendance of in-home groups is usually restricted to one – and there might be further restrictions, such as no males attending a female group, since the client is usually visible to the respondents. Interviewing in viewing facilities, or under observation changes the relationship between moderator and respondent. Both are aware there is a third party in the relationship and may change behaviour accordingly.

Figure 5.1 shows only a simplified version of the relationships that can arise in this situation. The closed group of moderator and respondents is opened up by the moderator's and respondents' awareness of the clients' presence. Since respondents sit facing the mirror, they can be continually reminded of the clients. (In practice, they do seem to be able to ignore the

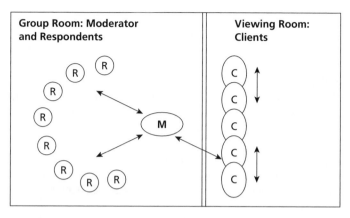

FIGURE 5.1  *Some of the relationships that arise in a viewing studio situation*

mirror for long periods of time; with some indulging in behaviours that indicate they have forgotten they are being watched.) Occasionally they lose eye contact with the moderator and address their points to the mirror. More often, they make points intended for the ears of the clients, such as complaining about high pricing or over-packaging, even if these are not on the research agenda.

The moderator has to be very careful in explaining the clients' presence as this could bias the findings. The MRS Code of Conduct requires transparency and honesty, but clients themselves are not always comfortable with being identified. Usually the description is to the effect that these people are involved in the project and have come to watch because the details of the research are very pertinent to their work. Some moderators will offer to introduce the clients personally to the group at the end of the research.

Moderators are largely correct if they feel their work is being judged. Clients attend to get more understanding of their target audience and personal insight into the research issues. However, there is also an element of quality control; checking if the recruitment quota is as specified, checking that the research materials are functioning as intended, and that the moderator is running the group 'well'. The difficulty arises when clients are not aware of all the factors involved in running a group well, and base their judgements on highly visible scenarios such as the moderator's ability to deal with a dominant respondent. Clients tend to be more pleased with the research process if the findings are positive, than if they are disappointed with the results.

There is a temptation for both moderator and respondents to make the group experience more theatrical and entertaining than a 'natural' group. 'Moderators learn that the drama in a discussion does not always reach the audience' (Checkman 1989: 36), and are tempted to encourage performance from the respondents – which can work against authenticity of response. Sometimes respondents need little encouragement to 'perform'. Groups of young women have tried to embarrass male viewers with sexually explicit banter and some teenagers will pull faces and make gestures at the mirror.

For clients, the mirror and TV screens have a blunting effect on involvement with the group; the immediacy and energy of the group is harder to appreciate, and there can be discrepancies between the moderator's perception of what makes a 'successful group' and how the clients judge it.

> all too often the creature comforts behind the screen, the voyeuristic nature of the experience and the politics of client/agency agendas interfere with the process of genuine open-minded listening. (Gordon 1997)

Robson and Wardle suggested that the general effect of viewing on responses was to make them more superficial and rational, and that the effects of observers are potentially exaggerated by the use of one-way mirrors. The observer 'is seen as judgemental and evaluative and respondents temper their contribution accordingly' (1988: 200). They made a number of suggestions for reducing and countering these effects, such as explaining observer roles fully as soon as possible, matching observers with groups and holding non-attended groups as a control. These are now implemented as part of the Market Research Society Qualitative Research Guidelines.

Another consideration in using viewing facilities is that they are a further step removed from the reality in which respondents' behaviour takes place.

> People in viewing rooms are observed away from their homes, shopping environments and neighbourhoods, which leads to a vacuum in which their verbal utterances take on meanings which do not reflect reality. (Gordon 1997)

There has not been a great deal of research on the impact of viewing on the research process, and existing findings tend to highlight the negatives. In the debates that surrounded the spread of viewing facilities in the UK, it was suggested that one reason some moderators disliked them was their own insecurity and defensiveness about having their work displayed (to an audience that did not appreciate the complexity of it).

There is a consistent increase in the number of groups held in facilities, as more and more clients want 'live access' to their target consumers. The facilities are certainly better equipped than the average suburban home and present a professional image which may be a benefit to some types of respondents. The evidence is that moderators have come to accept the mirror, and found ways of working to minimise the drawbacks of the situation. When clients listen well and appreciate the subtleties of the group situation, they can achieve a more intuitive and emotional appreciation of the findings than if they simply listened to the debrief. Although the mirror is a barrier, seeing some of their consumers can be more persuasive than hearing about them from a third party.

In the USA, the majority of groups are held in facilities, which are seen as providing a convenient and neutral ground for researcher and respondent to meet. Since the presence of a mirror is taken for granted it is less of an issue for US researchers, but they do have to put effort into 'dealing with the back room'. They give the respondents careful explanations about the set-up:

> I want to create a connection between the people in the focus group room and the people in the back room immediately, and I don't want them to think that anybody is observing without their knowledge, or that there is anything funny going on. (Moderator interview)

Some US clients will send in notes to the moderator asking for certain questions to be covered, and moderators everywhere routinely check with the client if anything else needs to be asked, during, or before the end, of the group. Sometimes another group forms in the back room after the research, in which the clients discuss the research. They can be distracted by particularly noticeable respondents, or be selectively looking for evidence to back up their view. In such cases, the wise moderator will use his or her skills to moderate this group as well.

> After the group I went into the client room and I said, 'OK I would like to capture what you learned'. I start off with this guy [who said] 'Oh I didn't learn anything, it just confirmed what I already knew.' So 'Didn't learn anything' I write on the board, and put his name next to it. Then I go round the room, and everyone else is like 'Wow, I learned this that and the other', and we came back round again. 'Well, I'd like to change mine; I did learn this and this is a new idea that was generated during the group.' (Moderator interview)

It might be noted that researchers everywhere also use their interviewing skills (subtly) in situations such as the research briefing, where they have to come to a clear understanding of what the client wants and expects from the research, and may have to 'interview' the client in order to establish this. (See Book 7, Chapter 5 for an example of this.)

## CONCLUSION

In summary, the interviewer–respondent relationship, brief though it is, is the foundation of interviewing and exists on many levels – the nonverbal, the social, the emotional, the intellectual, all of which influence each other simultaneously. It is bounded by the scope of research objectives, and influenced by the researcher–client relationship. The interviewer or the moderator has many choices about approach, style, the role(s) he or she can adopt, and the extent to which a cooperative or collaborative relationship is adopted with the respondents. Moderators need to have an awareness of how the process affects respondents, and when using viewing facilities, an awareness of how the setting affects them also. Research strongly suggests that overall quality of response would be much improved if moderators were able to take enough time to present material and techniques at a pace suitable for respondents to assess and integrate the material. This means researchers need to be more assertive when faced with over-long topic guides, and educate their clients that the extra questions will achieve little.

## KEY POINTS

- The quality of the interviewer makes a difference to the quality of the research output, as the interviewer is the research instrument. Although basic interviewing skills can be good enough for a simple project, researchers need training, experience and development to deal with the challenges and pitfalls of interviewing in a range of situations.
- Moderators may choose to play different roles but need to retain a core of authenticity, as respondents take their cues from the behaviour of the moderator.
- Interviewers should be aware of possible sources of bias, unintended communication, and imbalances of power, and should have explicit strategies in place to deal with these.
- Respondents are 'acutely sensitive' to the moderator at the start of the group, a critical period for setting expectations and patterns for group communication processes. Respondents understand the role of the moderator is to encourage equal contributions from everybody, and notice if the moderator fails to do so, is patronising or is clearly aiming at a particular conclusion.
- Moderators should be bolder in managing the group process; respondents give them the permission and the power to do so. There is a 'hidden contract' between interviewer and respondent. Once accepted by the respondent, he or she is keen to help in the process, but wants to be given clear guidance on what is required and why. Respondents are uncomfortable with situations where the interviewer is too non-directive, doesn't explain tasks and techniques adequately, and rushes through stimulus material.
- Groups are increasingly being held in viewing facilities, so that clients can see and hear the respondents at first hand. Moderators working in such facilities need to manage both the respondents' and the clients' expectations and participation in the process.
- Moderators need to re-evaluate the benefits of taking time to manage the group process effectively and resist the pressure by clients to fill up the topic guide.

# Planning an Interview or Group Discussion

Planning an interview involves more than working out a list of questions. The location of the research, and how it is designed and conducted, will create expectations that can affect responses.

The interview plan, usually known as a topic or discussion guide, looks like a straightforward list of questions, but is designed to deal with process issues as well as the content. It has both symbolic and practical significance in the qualitative market research process. It demonstrates the researcher's ability, understanding and methodological awareness, but it can become a battleground on which the power relationship between researcher and client is played out.

## VARIATIONS FOR DIFFERENT TYPES OF INTERVIEW

The objectives and sample determine the nature of preparation for the interviewing. Part of the preparation involves deciding on the venue and timing, a choice that will be affected by both practical and process reasons. The venue needs to be suitable for the type of respondent, offering both psychological and physical comfort. The timing of the interviews will also have implications for respondent's comfort – breaks, refreshments and overall length of the interview process.

The objectives dictate the length and mood of the group or interview, while use of some of the projective and enabling techniques requires pre-planning. The interviews might require the presence of a wide range of stimulus material representing various aspects of the subject under discussion, particularly when working with children. (Sometimes the group setting itself is the stimulus, if the subject of the research is a venue.)

The research materials, the structure and timing of the topic guide are appropriate to the subject; slow and thoughtful for difficult issues, fun and stimulating for creative groups. A research interview can look like a deep and meaningful discussion, or it can look more like a creative workshop, full of fun and laughter. The middle ground between these two is occupied by what many people might see as a 'typical' group; a suburban living room or viewing studio, with eight or so respondents sitting on armchairs, and discussing a range of issues for a couple of hours.

## STRUCTURE, PROCESS AND CONTENT

Process factors are the underlying patterns of interaction within the group – who talks with whom, what roles people adopt, etc. The content refers to the subject of the research; both the scope of the research topics and the findings of the research.

There is a third factor, which needs to be taken into account in planning, and that is the structure, meaning the physical location and layout of the place where the interviewing will happen.

### Structural Issues

In the UK, qualitative market research interviews and discussions typically take place in a recruiter's home, increasingly in viewing facilities. At other times, it makes sense to hold research in locations where the behaviour being studied actually takes place, or where the respondents will feel most comfortable. These might include hotels, town halls, drinking establishments, even Boy Scout huts. Sometimes hotels are chosen as they provide a central location for people coming from different areas. There are even mobile groups, which visit two or three locations in one session. Each of these locations has advantages and disadvantages, which relate to access of respondents, clients and interviewers, the facilities available, the space and privacy available at the location, and the cost.

Sometimes the choice is forced. If a number of clients need to attend on one night, it has to be a viewing facility. If there is no private facility or recruiter in the area a room in a hotel may need to be booked. If several computers are required online a specialist location will be needed. However, where the researcher has a choice, it should be based on enhancing the research process as much as possible. Creative groups work well in a setting like a nursery school, where respondents are surrounded by vibrant examples of uninhibited creativity. Food groups might be held round a dinner table, young people's groups in a youth club and so on. Such venues help the respondents to feel more at ease, and to bring back the feelings and experiences associated with them.

Even in the recruiter's living room, the room layout, height of the chairs and type of refreshments offered will signal to respondents what the expectations are about them. The type and layout of furniture affects the power relationships between moderator and respondents. Recruiters sometimes provide the largest and most comfortable chair for the moderator – a real 'head of household' chair – but often sitting in this chair will be counter-productive. It will not help to have a seating position where the group literally has to 'look up to' the moderator. It is best if the chairs are all of the same type, or even if the moderator can sit slightly lower. Importantly, the moderator needs to be able to make eye contact easily with everyone in the room, and may need to rearrange the furniture to do so. If a client is sitting in the room, they should be out of the line of sight of the respondents, because their facial reactions can indicate approval or disapproval of respondents' opinions.

In the USA, it is common to have respondents seated around a table, boardroom style, which is helpful for handling reading or writing materials. This is believed by American moderators to provide an element of 'protection', a comfort zone, as the lower half of the body is hidden. Without it, they believe, men in particular take longer to drop their defences. In viewing studios, UK moderators most often ask for an informal armchair seating layout with a coffee table in the centre, finding that boardroom style can make the session too formal.

For depth interviewing the best situation is to have chairs at 45° angles. Directly opposite is too confrontational, but sitting side by side seems less engaged. When the chairs are angled the interviewer can hold eye contact with the respondent or easily look away, allowing the respondent some thinking time and space.

Another structural issue is recording method. It is not possible for a moderator to take full notes and run a group at the same time, and note-taking would involve another person being in the room. Most commonly groups are audio-recorded, occasionally they might be video-recorded in a living room, and if they are in a viewing facility audio and video recordings are usually made.

The interviewer or moderator needs to show care and respect for the respondents by ensuring that all their physical needs are met, and including appropriate breaks in the process. Refreshments and breaks will also help maintain energy levels in the group.

### Process Issues

Everything the moderator does, and the way in which it is done, is taken by respondents, consciously or unconsciously, as a message about what is required from them and how they should behave. The Tuckman model of group development described in Chapter 4 clarifies in detail why this is so. A group passes through various stages in its formation and is not ready to work at certain types of task until the appropriate stage has been reached.

Practised moderators use an implicit *process guide,* their knowledge of the best order, timing and nature of tasks. They put this down to experience, empathy and intuition. Occasionally a client might ask for a complex evaluation task, say reactions to a commercial, to be done right at the start of the group 'to get spontaneous reactions without any bias'. The moderator will know that this will not work, or will produce results more akin to quantitative research, although he or she may not be able to explain the theoretical basis of it.

Therefore, in planning the content and strategy of the interview, the researcher has to plan to deal with process issues too. These will include:

- Devising a good introduction, warm-up exercise or session, and easy questions for the forming and norming stage. (A later section deals more specifically with the content of an introduction and the nature of a warm-up exercise.)
- Moderating power imbalances through the types of task that are set. This might include such strategies as sub-dividing the group to allocate responsibilities for exploring different aspects of the research issue before debating them as a whole.
- Using tasks and exercises that encourage appropriate channels of communication (usually respondent-to-respondent rather than respondent-to-moderator). Occasionally the opposite is required – when individual views need to be established, a pen and paper exercise encourages respondents to consolidate their own view before discussing it with others.
- Being aware of order effects, as discussion of one topic may affect reactions to a following one. There is also an education effect, so there may be a need to hold back information until a certain point is reached.
- Varying the nature of the questions and the tasks to maintain the flow of energy within the group, and varying the emotional tone of the group to reflect the subject matter.
- Closing the process to everyone's satisfaction.

### Content Issues

A very important distinction, albeit one that is becoming lost in practice, is between a focus group and a group discussion (Imms 1999). A focus group is much more prescribed in content. The moderator has to ensure that specific types of information are elicited, and has to keep the discussion between those boundaries; therefore quite a lot of semi-structured questions are needed, which are agreed beforehand with the client.

A group discussion is much more open-ended, allowing the respondents to discuss anything of relevance to the topic, and allows the moderator to use much more open-ended questioning and probing. Whereas the focus group provides information, the group discussion provides understanding.

> If the project is such that it requires a lot of depth, I tell the client up front this is not normal focus group research. (Moderator interview)

In practice, research projects can be a hybrid of the two. Most clients insist on seeing some form of topic or discussion guide prior to the start of the research, as this confirms to them that the researcher has a good understanding of the objectives. Moderators can then follow some parts precisely, but occasionally veer off topic to explore something of interest.

## THE ROLE OF THE TOPIC OR DISCUSSION GUIDE

At the planning stage of the research, the topic guide is a very important document.

1  It is a practical framework that delineates the boundaries of the research – what is to be excluded or included.
2  It becomes a forum for the formulation and exploration of initial hypotheses.
3  It is important in building the relationship with the client, showing competence, developing trust – and sometimes negotiating power.

### A Practical Framework

Much depends on the working knowledge the researcher has of the market, and on the ability of the client to provide a brief with relevant background information and a clear set of research questions. Where there is a long and close working relationship, the brief might consist of a telephone call asking a researcher to set up a project just like a previous one. Most researchers will at this point submit an outline proposal with sample, costs and an indication of what will be covered, but many will recall situations where a research project has gone ahead with no paperwork whatsoever. Even the objectives are not actually written down until it is time to report. This situation assumes a very high level of trust and knowledge.

At the other end of the scale, the development of the topic guide may be a painstaking process. The researcher may need to obtain background information on the market or establish more precisely what the client knows or believes. Sometimes there is a case for a brainstorming process to establish what else might be helpful or interesting to know. There may be a need to translate from the client's marketing objectives, often phrased in terms of brand share, distribution, competitive positionings and so on, into a consumer framework that is more related to usage, purchasing and brand image. To make the research both actionable and realistic, the researcher will ask how it will be used, and what regulatory and practical restrictions are in force.

An initial topic guide is used to test the congruence between the client's objectives and the researcher's proposals. This also clarifies the relative importance of the various objectives, and the client's comfort with the research approach.

### Formulation and Exploration of Initial Hypotheses

Some hypotheses only come to light when the actual questions to be used have to be written down. In this respect, the topic guide can be considered as one of the earlier stages of analysis. Client and researcher assumptions become clearer as the topics and stimulus material are developed. Clients sometimes offer lists of factors to be explored, which are sometimes based on previous research, or may be hypotheses about how marketing or communication factors work.

### Building the Relationship with the Client

There may be on-going discussions about stimulus material (products, written material, representations of new ideas) – what type, what degree of finish and whether what has been supplied will do the job. From the client's point of view, the topic guide and the stimulus material have major significance, because these are the physical representations of the research they can control. A number of different agencies may be involved – different teams from the client organisation, designers, project consultants, advertising agencies, public relations companies – and the topic guide is a means for obtaining consensus about the research.

In the US cognitive model, the topic guide is in effect a script for the researcher to follow and is structured to fit the client's needs, sometimes ignoring those of moderator and respondents. However in this case the moderator is likely to be hired for moderating duties only, and may not play a role in planning and analysis at all.

In the conative model, followed sometimes in the USA and most often in Europe, the researcher takes some or all of the responsibility for developing the topic guide. The researcher will be aiming to demonstrate understanding of the issues to the client, to fit questions and sections in at the appropriate stage, to develop some sort of useful or logical path through the material, and to include stimulus material and any specialist techniques. It is a statement of the researcher's competence.

At its best, a topic guide is a cooperative project between researcher and client and is a way of developing the relationship between them. By demonstrating his or her knowledge, the researcher builds trust in both themselves and the process. The ultimate form of the topic guide is to some extent a reflection of the power relationship between researcher and client.

> I make myself available to them as an equal team member and I advise them what to do. If they don't want to do it, that is their prerogative. (Moderator interview)

Researchers may develop long and detailed topic guides, which demonstrate to the client the value for money they are getting. This ends up being counter-productive as the research becomes rushed and the process suffers. Clients also seek value by adding more concepts, questions, or ideas than are necessary, seemingly unaware of the time needed to deal with subjects properly.

They don't want to test three concepts and probe why ... they want to squeeze in seven. In theory we try to peel the layers of the onion, but we have not been able to get at that level as much as we should. Talking to people from other research companies, that is across the board. (Moderator interview)

This can be a very delicate situation, but can be handled well:

Some [clients] need more guidance than others; some think they know more – which is OK, we let them go on with that belief, but what we are doing in the process is providing them with a lot of input they don't know about. (Moderator interview)

The consequence of not being experienced or assertive enough is to end up with an overloaded topic guide, making the discussion a rushed question and answer session rather than a meaningful dialogue. A good compromise solution is to use the first group or two as a 'pilot' session to check the amount of time for all the issues, and amend the topic guide accordingly.

## DEVISING A TOPIC GUIDE

Whether it is for an individual interview or a group, a topic guide usually has an introduction, a warm-up, a structure dictated by process issues and the content of the research, and a closing section.

### Introduction

A good introduction needs to include a welcome, a mention of the people and companies involved, and a disclosure of the purpose of the research – at this stage in outline. The role of the moderator and of the observers needs to be explained. Moderators who say it is their task to ensure everyone contributes equally give themselves permission to effectively manage the group process later. It is always worth repeating that individual opinions are valued and that disagreements are acceptable, as this works against group tendencies to consensus. Many moderators also say there are no right or wrong answers to assuage any concerns about competence to be a respondent.

Issues to do with recording methods, use of information, respondent anonymity and right to withdraw from the research need to be dealt with before the group starts. (Some guidelines suggest that these are best discussed during the recruitment process; this is especially so when viewing facilities are to be used, or in employee research, where anonymity may be an issue.)

Some moderators add that the recording is necessary as everyone's views are valuable. Housekeeping points such as timing, and the location of the toilets need to be included too. Interviewers have been known to become anxious about closed body language half way through an interview only to discover the respondent really wants to go to the toilet but won't say!

Note that the introduction communicates as much through the way it is said as the content itself. The degree of formality, naturalness, humour and the personality of the moderator will start to set the norms of the group. Aware moderators use this to their advantage, using their own behaviour to signal to respondents how they want them to behave.

### Warm-up

The introduction leads straight into the warm-up, which aims to get everybody talking as soon as possible, and to establish an individual moderator–respondent connection before the group forms. It also introduces the respondents to each other.

The most common form is to ask everyone to say something about his or her family, job, or social life, and/or to give some background details relevant to the topic of the research. Sometimes moderators don't want the research topic introduced and may choose to warm up by asking respondents about the area they live in, what interesting films or commercials people have seen recently, or asking what people would do if they won a million pounds.

A variation on this is the paired warm-up. Respondents are divided into pairs and have to interview each other briefly before introducing the other person to the rest of the group. This gives each person a 'buddy' and raises the initial energy level, but then further efforts are needed to bond the pairs into a group.

Many other options are available. If the group is to be a creative one, the simple expedient of offering respondents large coloured crayons to write their names with gets them in the mood. If the group is to be run workshop style, a warm-up game where the respondents have to interact and discover things about each other might be more suitable. A group that will require emotional disclosure might start by asking people to recount how they felt on their first ever day at school – an emotional topic but far enough away to be safe to discuss.

Respondents arrive at groups carrying a lot of emotional baggage, not only to do with their past experiences of being in all types of groups, but also baggage acquired during the day, their current concerns and stresses. Some moderators believe it helps to re-frame the respondents' mindset by starting them with a task that is pleasant and puts them into a positive mood, for example looking at pictures that remind them of good experiences they have had.

A degree of emotional safety is important during the warm-up process. After the initial exercise, the warm-up phase continues with simple questions that are easy for respondents to answer, until the moderator has a sense that the group has bonded. There is a close relationship between the types of question that are asked in the early stages of a group and the group process. Referring back to the adapted Tuckman model in Chapter 4, it will be seen that the role of the moderator at these stages is to deal with respondent anxieties, set appropriate group norms and prepare the group for the tasks ahead. Questions that might be perceived as difficult to answer tend to distract both the group and the moderator from this task.

### Structure of the Topic Guide

The basic principles are to start with the easier topics, get early information that will help with understanding later views and to be aware of order effects, which may educate or bias respondents by mentioning issues that come later. An awareness of group process will help to plan the timing and order of topics and techniques.

Many guides have the key overarching questions separated into topic areas, with particularly important prompts and probes. The usual path is from the general to the particular. Thus if the research is to explore non-financial remuneration for employees, the topics might include the nature of their work, what they find rewarding about it, what is frustrating about it, what beliefs there are about pay and conditions at other companies, how they feel when opening their pay packet, what incentive schemes do they know about and so on.

Depending on the objectives, the structure of the topic guide can be seen as a tree with many branches (many connected facets to explore), a river that flows through unknown territory (one main theme with many issues) or as a low-level flight in a small plane, picking out landmarks and hoping to find some landing lights. There are problems to be faced and trade-offs to be made. It helps to make clients aware that it is rarely as logical as it appears to be when set down on paper.

> I tell them a group is a lot like a tree. It is not linear by any means. I need to make sure I can go out on the branches as far as I can. The more branches [there are], I can't go out as far on any branch. (Moderator interview)

Sometimes it is possible and appropriate to structure the guide so that separate themes are explored and then come together in a grand finale as the key idea is revealed. Where it is suspected there may be order effects, segments of the guide need to be rotated or randomised; it is wise to routinely do this with stimulus material unless it needs to be presented in a specific order. However loose or structured the guide, there needs to be enough time for summarising at the end – a process helpful to all involved.

### Types of Question

There is some theory about the effects of different types of question. Krueger (1998), for example, describes opening, introductory, transition, key and ending questions. In the conative model, there is likely to be a difference between the questions listed and how those questions are actually asked. This comes from the experience and skill of the moderator, who adapts the questions as necessary. Krueger says the 'topic guide is more often used by people who do moderating for a living, and these experts have developed a sense of what will and won't work' (1998: 11). He recommends the 'questioning route' for inexperienced moderators, especially if they are sharing a project. By this, he means writing the questions out in full and following the planned order.

A novice research interviewer may well write out a number of questions in full. The process of developing and rehearsing them helps in using them more spontaneously. (It is distracting and dispiriting for respondents if the interviewer seems to be merely reading from a list of predetermined questions rather than following on from respondents' comments as they arise.) Mostly, it is impossible for a researcher to predict every question in advance. Many types of question do not appear on a topic guide. There is an understanding that there should be fluidity in the process; and once they have internalised the objectives, experienced interviewers rely on their acquired skills to frame the questions. Most qualitative market researchers are trained in the differences between open and closed questions, and in the usefulness of paraphrasing, summarising, reflecting and challenging. Researchers aim for a style that is not interrogatory, using 'why' very carefully and softening questions with introductory phrases like 'I'm interested in what you said about ...' or 'I noticed you ...' rather than asking a lot of who, what, why, where, when, how? questions. Each interviewer has a favourite repertoire of prompts and probes, encouraging signals, follow-up questions and challenges. An ideal qualitative interview is one in which relatively few direct questions are asked.

Interviewers or moderators will also use hypothetical 'what if' questions, provocative devil's advocate questions, ask for stories, examples, clarification of situations, words and phrases, and interactions of factors in a process such as purchasing. In addition, there are many techniques, ranging from simple lists and sorts to projective techniques, all of which have their specific types of question and sequence. (Chapters 7 and 8 describe these in more detail.)

### Building in Techniques

Qualitative interviewers have different ideas as to what constitutes a 'technique'. Some prefer to rely on straightforward, albeit subtle, questioning, while others run a group with what they call a series of 'games', which might include word association, producing competitive lists of positives and negatives, various ordering and sorting procedures, etc. Some researchers are comfortable with using numerical approaches (counting how many hold a certain view or using a scale of interest in purchase), while others prefer to avoid this, believing that clients might switch into a quantitative mindset if they see this happening.

There are some projective techniques such as personification (turning a product or brand into a person and describing their personality and lifestyle), which can be done on impulse. However, many of these techniques require some preparation, if only having crayons and paper ready, and some require significant amounts of time. It is important therefore that the researcher

- decides in advance what techniques may be useful;
- sets aside an appropriate amount of time in the guide – not just for the technique but for the newly-enriched discussion which will result;
- uses the technique at the appropriate stage in the group.

When the techniques are presented to respondents as 'games' or fun activities, it can also underestimate their value in the eyes of the client. Some researchers find it difficult to persuade clients it is worthwhile to use up group time on these whereas; those who are confident about the power and value of the techniques can make a better case.

### USING A TOPIC GUIDE IN PRACTICE

In the USA cognitive tradition (Goodyear 1996) the groups are run with up to 12 respondents, with a very structured procedure and sometimes with client participation from behind the mirror. In such a case, there is very little chance for the moderator to improvise. However, it must be appreciated that 'cognitive' moderators do have a skilled task to do, since they are a moment-by-moment bridge between clients and respondents and their attention has to be in two places at once.

However, other researchers in the USA work in the European conative style, being more exploratory, focusing on inner feelings and other forms of subtle or implicit material. This style allows the experienced moderator to set aside the topic guide, using it for occasional reference and as a check at the end. Some moderators will rewrite the topic guide into something that can be glanced at quickly during the group:

> I have my own guide and it is usually a piece of paper with seven or eight words on it, and I use my intuition or my experience, whatever you want to call it, to introduce exercises that are appropriate for what I am trying to get out of them. (Moderator interview)

This allows moderators to participate much more fully in the group. If they have written the guide, they will have internalised the objectives, and now they can give their full concentration to the process and content of the group. Constantly referring to a list of questions creates a barrier to flow.

Younger and less experienced moderators are more likely to rely on the topic guide, eventually moving further away from it as the project progresses. It gives them confidence, a back-up in case they get lost, and a checklist to make sure everything has been covered. Topic guides do often loosen up after the first few groups, when it is clear that some topics have obvious answers while others require a lot more exploration. Sometimes these changes are made in consultation with the client; sometimes it is left to the researcher. A benefit of a viewed group is that it allows joint decisions to be made about how the guide is working.

Another issue is the extent to which moderators feel free to go 'off topic'. Clients need to be able to trust that the moderator is exploring something worthwhile and that eventually its usefulness will become clear. This is much less of an issue if the client is not viewing the groups. Some clients expect the researcher to come back with something new and different, and actively encourage this process.

The prime importance of the topic guide is in the early stages of interviewing, and it is as much for managing the client relationship as it is for managing the respondent relationship. Once the research is under way and directions and findings are becoming clearer, client and researcher alike have more faith that the process will deliver what is required.

## CONCLUSION

The nature of qualitative market research presents a challenge when building the relationship with the client. It is the topic guide that has to persuade the client the research can indeed access the complex, emotional, intuitive, hidden, 'unconscious' world of the respondent. Clients are buying trust and reputation; there are no guarantees the research process will deliver amazing new insights. The process of planning and developing the guide has an important role in defining and grounding the research, as well as building trust in the expertise of the researcher.

**KEY POINTS**

- Planning of the interview or group needs to include the structure (location and layout), the content (the subjects to be included) and the process (type and order of questions and techniques).
- The interview or topic guide makes explicit initial hypotheses and assumptions, acts as a practical framework for the research, helps build the relationship with the client – and sometimes becomes a focal point for negotiation between all interested parties.
- A typical guide will include an introduction and warm-up, topics, techniques and stimulus material in the approximate order of use, and a summary or ending phase. It will take into account the development of group processes as well as possible biases introduced by the order in which questions are presented.
- Inexperienced moderators (and those who need to work in the US cognitive style) will have the detailed questions listed out and will follow them closely; other moderators prefer to internalise the objectives and frame their own questions through their involvement and interaction with the group.

# Interviewing Skills

This chapter aims to demystify some of the strategies and skills involved in what might be regarded as the essence of the interviewing process. It shows how the principles of non-directive interviewing have been adapted to enable exploration of the respondent's emotional, social and cultural world. Some strategies for enhancing the group process and dealing with 'difficult' respondents are outlined.

Interviewing skills include a large non-verbal component in building rapport, managing processes and power relationships. The interviewing process therefore occurs on many levels – physical and non-verbal, cognitive, emotional and intuitive.

## THE VIRTUOUS CIRCLE OF ELICITING AND LISTENING SKILLS

This is the core of the interviewing process, and is dependent on both listening and eliciting skills. (The term 'eliciting' is used rather than questioning, because it is often preferable to avoid direct questioning.) Commercial researchers use many ways to invite useful contributions. Listening and eliciting feed into one another, so the interview can follow and explore the respondent's view of the world. First eliciting and listening skills are described separately, then it can be seen how the two dovetail together.

### Eliciting Skills

The skills themselves are relatively neutral in that they support most kinds of theoretical orientations or perspectives. The content of the questions may be different if the researcher is working within a particular framework, but the ways in which topics are introduced and developed are essentially similar. The art of interviewing is to be clear and specific about the question forms that are chosen – and ultimately to ask as few direct questions as possible. Conversation analysis shows that most question–answer sequences happen in the larger scale, institutional contexts of social life, where there are often power imbalances and normative rules. Most respondents feel more comfortable using the freer types of interaction that occur in everyday conversation (Hutchby and Wooffitt 1998).

Basic questions are divided into **open questions** (who, what, why, where, when, how?), which lead to answers that are open-ended and descriptive, and **closed questions**, which often start with the form 'are', 'have', 'do/did?' The literal answer to a closed question is yes or no, although in conversation people may go on to justify this answer.

Both types of question are useful in qualitative research. Closed questions establish basic information quickly, and open questions allow the interviewer to ask about a topic area without limiting the response. Closed questions may be used as a form of summary to check understanding, and signal the end of the conversation. Problems arise when novice interviewers habitually use closed questions without thinking. An extrovert respondent may ignore them, but a quiet respondent will not be encouraged to open up. A series of closed questions can be leading, as it gives away the interviewer's agenda. Too many closed questions give the impression that the interviewer is just information-gathering and demotivate the respondent.

Interviewers soften their open questions by indicating they are curious, interested, wondering about how the respondent feels about the issue. (In NLP, these are called **embedded questions** – the question being embedded within the listener's curiosity.) The question becomes 'I am wondering how you came to get involved in ...' rather than 'How did you get involved in ...' This is particularly important when asking 'why', because 'why' questions can sound interrogative and challenging. They encourage post-rationalisations, as consumers feel a need to explain and justify their behaviour. Instead of 'Why did you choose that policy?', ' I'm curious as to why you chose that policy?' Even better to rephrase it into a more specific question: 'What is it about that policy that interested you?' or 'What were the different things you considered when choosing the policy?'

As the respondent continues the interviewer may use signals of encouragement to show they are listening ('Aha', 'Go on'), and will often use **prompts** to encourage further description – 'tell me more', 'please explain that part', 'what happened then?', and so on. There are also probes to ensure the respondent has not left out anything of importance. Most often used ones are 'what else?' (which has the inbuilt assumption that there is something else) and 'is there anything else?'. There are many more encouraging non-verbal signals too, the most common being nodding while listening. In a group the moderator will encourage responses from other respondents, with prompts such as 'What do other people feel about that?' or 'What other views are there?'

Some interviewers and group moderators believe in verbally rewarding contributions from the respondents, saying 'that's great', 'that's really interesting', 'this is the sort of stuff we need to know'. This is helpful in encouraging less confident respondents and people who really are not clear whether their discussion of the shade of green on a brochure is being at all helpful. However, moderators need to use these carefully, as an unconscious pattern of usage can end up being leading. They may reward people who offer information that agrees with the moderator's hypothesis, but not say 'that's great' to the others.

The more powerful (and neutral or non-directive) eliciting skills include echoing, paraphrasing, reflecting and summarising. **Echoing** is simply picking out a critical word or phrase used by the respondent, in a questioning tone of voice. It works very well when used occasionally, as it hardly interrupts the flow.

> *Respondent:* When I got it home and there were about 20 pages of instructions, I felt quite intimidated.
> *Interviewer:* Intimidated?

It can become irritating if used a lot, so another option is to **paraphrase**, often using a form such as 'What you seem to be saying is …' Nothing is added by paraphrasing, yet the respondent feels understood and will often go on to disclose a great deal more. Just hearing the moderator repeat their views seems to provide validation and encouragement.

**Reflecting** is like paraphrasing, but it picks out the emotional content. An interviewer might say 'You have described a lot of frustrations with the poor service; I got the impression there may be some anger there as well?' The question mark is an indication that this interpretation is offered to the respondent to confirm or deny before the interview proceeds further. For interviewers and moderators who want to work on an emotional level as much as possible, reflecting is the key skill to practise. Successful reflecting relies on listening to the message that is underneath the words, and sensitivity to the respondent's emotional state. It does not have to be done very often, but it is powerful because it immediately shifts the interview to a deeper level – assuming the respondent acknowledges and is willing to discuss the emotion.

**Summarising** has benefits for both interviewer and respondent. Respondents feel their point of view has been taken on board, and will often correct anything that has not come across as they intended. Some moderators deliberately summarise in a slightly hesitant manner, so that respondents have time to contribute and correct the summary. Summarising makes everyone concerned feel they have achieved something, reminds them of what has been covered, and signposts the ends of topics. Interviewers who are stuck for a question are advised to summarise, as the change to a different level of thinking reinstates research priorities. Moderators who don't summarise will end up with a group saying, 'Were we all right? Did we tell you what you needed to know?'

**Challenging** is an important part of interviewing. It includes challenging difficult roles in the group, for example the die-hard cynic or negator, challenging statements that seem exaggerated or unrealistic, and picking up discontinuities – 'I'm confused, because earlier you were saying X, now you seem to be saying Y?' Challenging works most successfully when the interviewer accepts that the confusion is theirs, and does not blame or judge the respondent for being inconsistent. Another way of challenging is to play devil's advocate ('What if I told you that …') or to bring in opposing information attributed to another source: 'People I spoke to last week were saying that it *is* possible to involve residents in these decisions as long as you have some sort of communication.'

Interviewers can spend a lot of time **clarifying**. 'When you say … what do you mean by …?' It may be necessary to clarify the usage of certain words, or to analyse entire concepts: 'So what specifically would "good service" mean to you?' Another way to do this would be to ask for specific examples.

An important part of using eliciting skills is being able to come up with the right intervention at the right time, and to keep things as simple as possible. This is why it looks so easy. Novice interviewers find they have a smaller repertoire of questions, they get stuck occasionally, and they find it hard to listen while formulating the next question. They also tend to ask too many questions at once, fearing the initial question has not been understood. They forget that respondents may need time to put feelings into words and to structure their thoughts before they say them aloud. Practice and increasing confidence help overcome these difficulties. The confident interviewer will feel able to share any difficulties he or she has in formulating questions with the group: 'I don't know quite how I am going to ask you this.' A helpful respondent or group will cooperate in defining the question as well as offering the answer!

### Listening Skills

It is often said that listening is an active process, but many people do not realise just how much energy and concentration it takes until they have to listen deeply to eight people for 2 hours. The processes of listening, picking up key words and phrases for reflecting, noticing who is contributing and who isn't, matching the content of the group against the objectives, and formulating hypotheses, require so much concentration they seem to produce an altered state of consciousness in the moderator. In this state of deep concentration, time can flow very quickly and seems condensed.

Listening is a form of selective translation. It is selective because the interviewer has to choose to listen in the first place, and may listen to only parts of what the respondent is saying. Many blocks to listening can get in the way. The listener may hear mainly what he or she wants to hear – a very good reason for listening to tapes or reading transcripts afterwards. The listener puts the meaning into his or her own frame of reference, sometimes unconsciously substituting concepts with slightly different meanings.

It is hard to listen when the significance and meaning of the words is not clear. Technical words or regional sayings need to be clarified and understood at the start. A degree of respect for the speaker is required. Interviewers who find their respondents offensive have to test their unconditional positive regard (see Carl Rogers in Chapter 4) and avoid judging people by their behaviour. Other blocks to listening include: making comparisons or even identifying with the respondent, labelling, rehearsing the next question, filtering out 'boring' bits, offering advice, joking off or sparring, correcting or advising the respondent, or worrying about whether the respondent likes the interviewer enough. All these blocks happen when the interviewer's own thoughts and concerns intrude. Sometimes personal agendas can lead to very selective listening and the use of leading questions as follow-ups, such as 'So would you say that ...?' (This might seem similar to reflecting, but it is getting the respondent to agree with the interviewer's agenda, whereas reflecting aims to deepen the understanding of the respondent's agenda.)

Training in listening skills involves a series of exercises that focus on different aspects of listening. Being able to hear and understand detailed content is important, as well as recognising verbal and non-verbal cues that an emotionally significant topic may have been touched on. Researchers have to make judgements about emotional engagement, commitment and the will of the respondent, and need to be aware what cues they personally use to do this. It is summed up by the thought: 'Listen to the music as well as the words.'

A simple but key skill is to appreciate the power of silence. Silences tend to panic novice moderators. Both researchers and clients have the idea that a 'good' group is a talkative, noisy, lively group. The silence is more uncomfortable for the moderator, as the respondents may be preparing answers or ruminating about the topic. The value of silence is that it is often broken with a thoughtful comment. An allied skill is to practise a 2 second silence before replying to a respondent, as this gives enough time to truly listen and integrate what is being said.

Apart from listening to content – the story the respondent tells, the opinion he or she gives – the interviewer listens to details of the language, and the way in which things are said. For example, a respondent might be describing the simple routines of having breakfast, and say something like 'I always put the milk in a jug, even when I am in a rush, because in our house you don't put milk bottles on the table.' The 'you' here is picked up by the interviewer as referring to some sort of code of behaviour, so the interviewer might frame a question about why milk bottles shouldn't be on tables and what it would signify if they were. The interviewer would then make careful use of the word 'people', signifying 'people not like me' as in: 'What sort of people do put milk bottles on tables?' Through good listening, a simple question about behaviour generates answers about belief systems and values. At other times, the interviewer will notice *how* a respondent is saying something. Is it on a social

| Deletion | *'I was always told that ...'* | Told by whom? |
|----------|-------------------------------|---------------|
| Lack of referential index | *'They're always in my way'* | Who/what specifically is always in your way? |
| Unspecified verb | *'He really frustrates me'* | How, specifically? |
| Nominalisations | *'I don't have the freedom'* | Free to do what? |

FIGURE 7.1    *Listening for what is left out: examples from NLP*

chit-chat level? Does it sound confessional? Was it said spontaneously or after an intervention? What mood and energy does it have? Elements like these contribute to the 'intuition' that good interviewers seem to display when in full flow.

It should be clear that an interviewer or moderator has to be motivated to listen well. This can be difficult when working with a long series of groups or depth interviews that cover the same subjects and don't evolve very much. The interviewer needs to have a strategy to recreate his or her own interest in the topic and the person. One strategy is to look out specifically for what is new and different; another is to remember that under the surface people have very different stories to tell and everyone is unique. Interviewers who use NLP (Neuro-Linguistic Programming, see Chapter 4) are able to recreate an optimal resource state – bring back a physical and mental state from a time when they were fascinated and engaged by an interview.

NLP also offers some strategies for good listening. One is listening for what is left out – non-specific nouns and verbs, distortions, deletions and generalisations made by respondents (see Figure 7.1). Abstract nouns, or 'fat words', are non-specific and tend to have many layers of meaning. 'Productivity', 'satisfaction', 'wealth' will mean very different things to different people – which is exactly why they are often used by politicians and other communicators. Listeners have to put their own interpretation into the words. The interviewer needs to unpack this process, by the simple technique of asking what the person would see, hear and feel when they were productive, satisfied, or wealthy. This sensory-based data is lean and specific, and makes it quite clear how specific experiences may vary. Hearing modal operators (should, ought, must, can't) indicates rules that may or may not be legitimate and can be challenged.

While being aware of such techniques helps, the ability to listen well requires some self-knowledge. Interviewers need to be aware of their usual blocks to listening, their likely biases and judgements, and they have to set aside their own thoughts and concerns. This ability is a life skill that contributes to better relationships in both business and personal life.

## *Integrating Eliciting and Listening Skills*

An interviewer needs to follow the content of what is being said, listen to the meaning underneath the words, and then gently bring this into the conversation. He or she offers or reflects back what they have heard, so that the respondent can confirm, deny, or elaborate. This way of working creates empathy, deepens the conversation and ensures the meaning has been understood.

These eliciting skills are non-directive in the sense that they follow the respondent. They use his or her language and concepts, they elaborate on issues of importance to the respondent, and it is clearly understood that the interviewer is aiming to understand and describe the world of the respondent. It is also part of the process of hypothesis creation. The words the interviewer chooses to pick out for echoing or reflection are ones that seem also to have some significance in terms of the objectives of the research. So the interview is gently guided from moment to moment within the framework of the research criteria.

It should be repeated that qualitative market researchers do not use true non-directive interviewing. The topics and questions of the topic guide focus the respondent in a particular direction. Indeed respondents are uncomfortable with an interviewer who is too neutral or non-directive, as they don't know what they should be discussing.

## GROUP FORMATION AND CONTROL

### *Strategies for Enhancing the Group or Interview*

Although researchers' questions seem to be about the content of the research, they are partially aimed at influencing and controlling the process of the group.

At the start of the interview, the questions are very simple, so respondents overcome any anxieties about the process and become more confident. In a group the moderator may use **inclusive questions** to encourage group formation – 'Does everybody ...?' – and make summaries which enhance the similarities between respondents by chunking up to whatever they have in common: 'You have told me that you go to very different places to get your vegetables, but you all seem to be looking for convenience and freshness in some way.'

Once respondents are settled in the group, individual differences start to become clearer, and the moderator takes account of these to work against the group tendency to consensus. A question might have a preamble about different viewpoints that have already been expressed: 'Christine says she usually gets good service at the bank, but Hannah has had some bad experiences. I wonder what experiences other people here have had?' Questions like this signal that a whole range of responses will be valued and that it is acceptable to bring up criticisms.

Another way of emphasising the value of individual responses is to set minor tasks, such as asking people to write down individually what they received from a communication before it is discussed in the group.

**Shared language** validates respondents' view of the world. The interviewer finds out what language respondents use to describe or categorise the products, and uses it him or herself: 'So when you are buying what you call "nibbly bits", how is that different from choosing "snacky things"?' The interviewer should acknowledge the language comes from the respondents, otherwise it can sound patronising. However, even this is far better than using the clients' terminology, which may include words like 'super-premium', 'extruded', or 'grab-bag'.

Researchers may take temporary sides in a discussion, although they usually signal this is for a good reason. It is usually to *support* a new idea, product, or commercial, which may be inadequately expressed by the stimulus material: 'I don't think you have given this one a fair hearing, so let's look again at its good points.' Occasionally the moderator may temporarily support a minority view amongst respondents, again to provide a balance.

**Signposting** is telling the respondents what is about to happen: 'We have just been talking about the Internet, and now we are going to move on to what people feel about buying music from websites.' This both helps prepare respondents for a slightly different topic, and helps alleviate any anxiety or concern about what may happen next.

**Summarising** similarly has both process and content benefits; it checks the accuracy of the content while making respondents feel their contribution has been very worthwhile.

### Strategies for Dealing with Difficult Groups or Respondents

Every group is unique and therefore unpredictable, and inevitably, some groups are harder to work with than others. There are different ideas about what constitutes a difficult group.

From a client viewer's perspective, quiet groups, where respondents seem less articulate and involved in the process, are often seen as difficult. Clients can fail to realise that a great deal of talking, laughter and high energy participation is not necessarily the route to the insights they are searching for. Inarticulate people may have different ways of expressing themselves and the actual information content may be the same, once all the extraneous jokiness has been stripped out of the entertaining group.

Clients also sometimes take the moderator's role a little too literally, feeling that there must be absolutely equal contributions from everybody. They may not be aware that groups need to have leaders, and that they have different types of leader; emotional leaders, task leaders, process leaders and so on. They become very nervous at any signs of dominance or leadership from one of the respondents, without noticing that respondents feel quite free to disagree with the views being expressed by this person.

These issues do reflect the anxieties that moderators have, since their most common 'difficult' respondents are the over-talkative ones, who do seem to take the group over, and the quiet ones, who contribute too little.

> In most groups you always have somebody who talks more than other people. That is my biggest problem. You have people who don't talk enough and people who talk too much. I don't want to say something verbally like 'don't talk so much'. That would be the worst thing I could do. (Moderator interview)

Each of these types of difficult respondent comes in different varieties. The over-talkative ones include those who seem impervious to the normal social signals that they should stop, the ones who tell long and irrelevant stories, the know-it-alls, and the ones who always leap in with an answer while everybody else is still listening to the question. The quiet ones include those who seem genuinely shy, come across as bored, or are 'lazy' – they are just there for the money and don't want to contribute.

It helps to consider why these people are being 'difficult'. Some clearly think they are helping the moderator; others might find they fear loss of influence and therefore use expertise, ingratiation, evasion, or even disengagement as strategies for getting attention. Some may be simply shy, bored, or more concerned with important life events happening outside the group. If they have not been well recruited they may not have the same degree of involvement with the topic.

Most moderators know the basic rules for dealing with these respondents. They know to start with non-verbal signals, such as refusing eye contact with the talkers and looking encouragingly at the quiet ones. They can turn their body or use subtle hand gestures to block one speaker and encourage another to speak. They can then use closed questions to summarise and close down the wafflers, and open questions addressed to the quiet respondents. Yet they do occasionally let things get out of control, and there are four main reasons for this.

1  They try to take control too late in the group process. The signs of potential process problems appear in the earlier stages, but moderators sometimes ignore them, hoping they will go away. Making efforts to encourage equal contributions early on pays dividends, as it then becomes one of the group norms.

2  They don't use names. It is very hard to remember 16 different names every night, and there is some feeling that it makes the group feel safer and more anonymous if names are not routinely used (although first

names are usually asked for at the start). It is worth the effort to devise a system of remembering names, as it is much easier then to pick out a respondent: 'Martin – what do feel about this?' sounds a lot better than 'You on the end of the sofa – what do you feel about this?'

3   They feel that it is rude to stop someone talking and intrusive to make a quiet person say something, and that the group will judge them negatively. This is about the moderator's need to be liked. What they don't realise is that the group are equally irritated by this difficult behaviour, and that they *expect* the moderator to handle this situation for them. The other members of the group are losing out, so they will like the moderator more for dealing with the situation rather than letting it go.

4   They fail to give themselves the power to intervene in the introduction. A simple statement such as 'I'm here to make sure everyone gets a chance to talk' during the introduction, allows them to say later 'As I said earlier, I need to make sure I get opinions from everybody, so now I would like to hear from the others.'

The type of statement in point 4 above enables the over-talkatives in the group to realise they are taking up group time, and offers a *carte blanche* to quieter respondents. There are other situations where a similar verbal statement can be more powerful than all the non-verbal gestures put together. Respondents who are talking amongst themselves (off topic) or a rowdy group can be stopped with something like 'Can people not all talk at once? I won't be able to hear all your views on the tape.'

Dominant respondents who have knowledge power (they talk a lot because they know the most) can be flattered into refraining from giving all their views by suggesting that the moderator needs to talk with the more typical consumers before having the benefit of their expertise. Those who leap in with immediate answers can be restrained by asking the group not to let them do all the work.

Those who are cynics, saboteurs, or soapboxers (they come to the research to use it as a forum for their views and make their point repeatedly) need to have their views acknowledged and validated but then ring-fenced by pointing out that there are many different views on the topic. The moderator can understand their point of view, but is also aware that there is a range of equally valid views, some of which may be held by other people in the group. (Another option is to distract them with a task, such as writing notes on a flip chart.)

Quiet respondents are harder to deal with in some ways. In a depth interview, the researcher can match the respondent's own quiet style, building confidence without pressure and allowing the respondent plenty of time to answer questions. In a group, opportunities for this are limited, and the moderator can only check with the respondent by name every so often about their position on a particular subject. Another strategy is to divide the group into pairs to discuss something amongst themselves, and then pick the quiet person from the pair to report back. Sometimes people may be quiet because they are not very verbal, and a change of task to a visual one will give them a chance to express themselves more confidently.

In the rare cases where a group becomes very difficult, the bold researcher can use meta-comment – comment on the process of the group. This involves stopping discussion about the content, making everyone in the group aware that something is wrong, and that the group needs to decide what to do about it. Researchers who also do group facilitation will be more comfortable with this idea, knowing that confronting the problem may be more painful but will be more effective than wasting a group discussion. Moderators should also acknowledge their own feelings about having to deal with such situations – the sense of loneliness, frustration, powerlessness, anger and confusion, otherwise these can build up and make further encounters more stressful.

## NON-VERBAL COMMUNICATION

One layer of non-verbal communication has already been described in the section on the physical structure of group surroundings in Chapter 6. The location and layout of the room signals expectations of the group process, and is useful in dealing with power inequalities.

Video tapes of groups show the importance and significance of **body language**. Moderators who sit still, hold their topic guide in front as a barrier, and use a monotonous tone of voice, are more likely to end up with groups that seem to lack vitality, energy and interest. In moderating training, one group is sometimes moderated by a series of different people, and it is extraordinary to watch the group energy change to match each moderator's style and energy.

Best practice is to be a flexible moderator, who is aware of the effect body language might have. For example, leaning forward to show listening with great attention; leaning back when wanting to stay out of the discussion. Sitting low and close to respondents encourages a more intimate, confessional atmosphere; standing up is a good way of taking charge of a group that needs some control. This is another reason why moderators put down their topic guide – constantly holding it inhibits freedom of movement.

No specialised knowledge of body language is needed. In a group, it is clusters of positions and gestures that are evident. People sit very quietly and separately in the forming stage of the group. As it warms up, they spread out, take more space, adopt more individual positions, and look more relaxed. By the performing stage they may be sitting forward, handling the stimulus material, looking much more animated. As the mourning stage starts, they will sit back in the chairs again, but this time with a sense of slow disengagement. Moderators notice anyone whose body language is significantly different from the others, and people who seem incongruent – that is, they might be saying something positive but displaying an uninterested posture. In line with the principles of the Humanistic approach, most moderators will find a way of checking out their interpretation of the body language by reflecting – 'I'm getting a sense that maybe you are not as keen on it as you say?'

Body language is one of the main ways of creating rapport. Rapport can be created by common interests in subject matter, but there is also a strong non-verbal element. It is based on the principle that people like others whom they perceive as similar – they feel more comfortable with what they know. Therefore, if people adopt similar body postures, rates and types of speech, rapport can be increased. The non-verbal experience of rapport is in fact created by synchronisation in tone, tempo and style, of physiology, body movements, sensory system and linguistic style.

Most interviewers almost unconsciously match the style of the respondents. NLP has made a study of the processes of rapport in detail, showing many variables that can be mirrored and matched. People have a subconscious awareness of others' physiological signs, such as rate and position of breathing, blink rate and degrees of tension in shoulders and facial muscles. These provide a very subtle level for matching, and are only possible to work with in depth interviews. Easier to work with are the overt body positions and movements that people make; crossing legs and arms, playing about with pencils, rubbing their noses or their knees, and smoothing their hair. The speed and style of these can be mirrored using complementary movements – this is important, otherwise the person feels they are being copied and feels foolish. People do not consciously notice that their conversational partner's foot might be moving at a similar rate to their hand, but the more alignment there is, the more comfortable they feel. Pitch and tone of voice gives further opportunities for matching, especially important in depth interviews, and key in telephone interviews. But even in a group situation, there are opportunities for the moderator to adopt the predominant style, whether it is upbeat and lively or slow and thoughtful.

Finally NLP suggests that people may process information in different ways, having different preferred representational systems:

| | |
|---|---|
| **Visual** | 'I *see* what you mean' |
| **Auditory** | 'I *hear* what you are saying' |
| **Kinaesthetic** | 'That *feels* right to me' |

The interviewer may pick up cues to somebody's preferred sensory system from the language they use (eye movements are another type of cue), and use the opportunity to build rapport further by using the same sensory system.

*Respondent:*   I see it quite differently
*Interviewer:*    How does it appear to you?

This question would be better than 'How do you feel about it' or 'I hear what you are saying; what is your grasp of the situation?'

While this seems very complex to learn, it is likely that many good moderators and interviewers use some of these skills naturally. This aspect of NLP was developed from detailed studies of great communicators and therapists who excelled in their ability to create rapport with others, and is a formalisation of the processes that occur. The system is dynamic. Once rapport is achieved through mirroring and matching, the interviewer can change the pace and energy of respondents through taking the lead (a process called pacing and leading), and this is a very useful tool for varying energy levels in long group sessions.

## WORKING AT DIFFERENT LEVELS

It should by now be clear that interviewing is very much more than a verbal process. An interviewer or a group moderator will be working at a physical level, taking care of the physical needs of the group, using physical structures and body language to send signals about the nature and intent of the research. According to Gorden (1980, in Fontana and Frey, 1994), the four main types of non-verbal communication in the interview context are:

- **Proxemic:** the use of space
- **Chronemic:** the use of timing in the pacing of speech and silences
- **Kinesic:** body movements and postures
- **Paralinguistic:** variation in volume, pitch and quality of voice.

From the outside, the thinking level can be clearly observed, as the sharing and exploration of ideas and issues progresses. A casual observer may not be aware of how that process in gently guided between the requirements of the research objectives and the need to understand the world the respondents live in.

The group also works on an emotional level. Whether or not the content appears to be emotional, the group process involves dealing with issues about belonging, dominance, self-assertion and position in a group. Sometimes there is an overt emotional content; there may be a cathartic effect as people discuss things they have not had a chance to speak about before, or a chance to vent anger or frustration – all of which must be managed by the moderator.

Then there is the intuitive/energy/synergistic level: noticing shifts in mood and energy, a sense of discovery, the role the whole group plays in producing the insights, and the mutual sense of satisfaction in a job well done.

## CONCLUSION

The skills and strategies of interviewing are not mysterious – they are founded on a knowledge base of how people are likely to react to questions and probes, and how they interact in dyads and groups. Rather, the mystery may be the ability of the interviewer to concentrate wholeheartedly on the full meaning of what respondents say, noting its implications for the objectives and the group process, simultaneously framing questions to develop it further, building the relationship with the respondents, and all the while consciously staying within the context of the research. (Chapter 1 aims to give insight into how all these processes are integrated and managed, as a set of moment-by-moment interviewer choices.)

### KEY POINTS

- Qualitative market research interviewers and moderators use a range of direct questions, prompts, probes and embedded questions as well as eliciting techniques such as paraphrasing and reflecting.
- Listening well is an active and intensive process that is rewarding because it opens up the respondents' emotional, social and cultural world. Moderators listen not only to what is said (and what is left out or implied), but also to how it is said. Interviewers have to be aware of their own blocks to listening and have respect for the respondent. NLP offers additional strategies for effective listening.
- Through the 'virtuous circle' of active listening and gentle eliciting skills, the interviewer can come to a deep understanding of the research issues through the respondent's frame of reference.
- Moderators choose particular types of question and intervention at different stages of the group process, to enable the smooth running of that process.
- 'Difficult' respondents or roles do appear in groups. Best practice is to prepare for this eventuality from the start: pick up the signs early, and be firm in using the strategies available for dealing with them. Many moderators do not realise the extent to which the group would support their intervention.
- The importance of non-verbal communication shows that interviewing is about managing an interactive process on many levels: physical, cognitive, emotional, intuitive and energetic. It can be challenging and demanding as well as rewarding.

# Enhancing the Interview with Stimulus Material and Projective Techniques

Qualitative commercial research has to be cost-effective. It has to meet the objectives, provide the depth of understanding required and provide actionable results within a budget and time frame. There is not the luxury of doing another set of interviews if the first one has not provided enough information or insight.

This chapter describes how qualitative market researchers augment their interviewing skills with the use of stimulus material and projective techniques to meet this challenge. Both of these involve, stimulate and focus respondents on key issues without restricting openness of response. Both work to some extent with non-conscious processes, encouraging and enabling respondents to talk about things they may never have thought of before, or didn't know they knew. Some ask the respondent to think differently or to work in a non-verbal modality. The techniques can reveal not only individual and social processes, but cultural assumptions as well.

## STIMULUS MATERIAL

### Roles and Types of Stimulus Material

Somewhat tautologously, stimulus material is defined as anything that has the specific purpose of stimulating discussion. This would include: packs, logos, brochures, descriptions of new ideas, materials intended to represent moods or need states and so on. Stimulus material has a number of specific roles:

- Involving and stimulating respondents prior to the research.
- Speeding up group formation and making the interviewing process easier by concretising issues.
- Enabling respondents to say more about the subject by providing visual and auditory cues.

- Representing ideas, products and commercials, which do not yet exist, in order to discuss reactions.

We shall look at each in turn.

One can *involve and stimulate respondents prior to the research* by tasking them to find or create material which they bring to the groups. This could include finding an object, texture, or a piece of music that represents how they feel when showering or eating a certain brand of chocolate. It might be something that documents their life and behaviour, a diary of eating patterns, photographs of their home and its surroundings, their favourite shoes or record albums.

These are several ways of *speeding up the process of group formation* and providing visual, auditory and tactile representations to supplant the verbal nature of the discussion. This commonly includes examples of the products being researched; or brochures, logos and photographs that might represent the organisation and its services. One of the most useful techniques is known as brand or product mapping, and involves asking the respondents to group together packs or logos '*in whatever ways they go together*'.

The group members will suddenly forget all their personal issues and anxieties, lean forward, get involved, move all the packs around, and by the time they have finished, feel they have achieved something together. Not only have they speeded up the process of forming, but also in describing the categories they used for mapping, the respondents will give the moderator the appropriate language for working in that category. The advantages of product mapping are summarised in Box 8.1.

---

### Box 8.1  The Advantages of Product Mapping

- Literally and physically maps a respondent's view of a product category or market

- Physically arranging the products or logos enables exploration of the relationships between them

- Can be simple and spontaneous; can be directed to cover specific issues

- Can be used in the early stages of a group

- Involves the respondent and works even with a verbally inexpressive respondent

- Requires only products or logos

---

A simple mapping exercise achieves an understanding of:

- Consumer/user vocabulary

- On what basis respondents/consumers discriminate/categorise

- The significance of packaging cues in this market

- What aspects of the brand/product contribute to its positioning

- What other products are regarded as competitive

- Possible market gaps

- Where new products or brand extensions may sit in the market

In working with children and young people a lot of stimulus material helps to make words and concepts concrete to them, and to keep them involved. Children may have very little to say about a piece of packaging in abstract, but ask them to draw it, and they will concentrate on the topic for several minutes. This is sometimes true of young adults as well, who have been brought up in a visually dominant world and have learnt to extract information from pictures through parallel processing rather better than through the serial processing of words.

Some stimulus material is brought into the research with the specific objective of *enabling respondents to say more about the subject*. This material becomes a focus for examination, and enables the interviewer to under-stand all its aspects in a relatively short space of time. The material triggers cues and associations, giving a richer response than unprompted ques-tions. It can be material that is already available, or be created specifically to explore aspects of an issue. An example of the latter would be a 'mood board', a collage of images chosen to represent a particular theme, feeling secure for example, or what freshness means to people. Such boards might be used to explore different aspects of a subject; for example, drinking coffee alone versus drinking it in a sociable environment. People first relate to the images, then access the feeling or mood, and discuss the implications of this in relation to their own experience. A purely verbal discussion would get there eventually, but this is a surer and faster process.

The final role of stimulus material is *to present products, services and ideas, which do not yet exist, in a tangible form, in order to discuss reactions*. This can be controversial, especially when researching creative ideas for advertis-ing, because there is often a gap between the expression of the idea and how it would appear in reality. This type of stimulus can appear in many

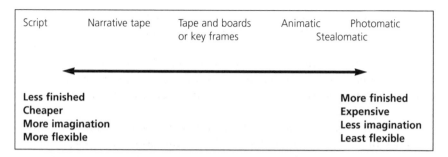

FIGURE 8.1   *Types of advertising research stimulus material*

forms. There is the written concept, usually an expression of a consumer insight about a problem, offering the product or service as a solution, rounded off with a consumer benefit. Sometimes the concept might have a picture attached, or be based mainly on a visualisation of the product. New packaging can be mocked up to various degrees of finish, and be two- or three-dimensional.

TV advertising, being multi-sensory, is particularly difficult to represent as stimulus material. Researchers have the choice of using mood boards, storyboards, key frames, animatics, photomatics, stealomatics, scripts, narrative tapes, radio 'interviews', mood music and any number of other options, either solo or in combination. Each has its advantages and disadvantages, and the choice is difficult. Trade-offs have to be made. Some researchers prefer to work at the 'less finished' end of the scale (see below) as it allows more flexibility and creativity and there is less likelihood of respondents getting over-involved with unimportant details. Others would rather work with something that looks as much like the finished product as possible.

Animatics are drawn pictures representing key frames from the story, which are filmed to give an illusion of movement. Animatics are good at integrating pictures, music and voiceover, and are useful for stories that are quite complicated. They give a better sense of how an ad happens in real time. Using an animatic guarantees that the stimulus will be presented the same way every time. However, they can look like cartoons and sometimes do not flow very easily. Characters with some depth to them may be hard to convey. A photomatic is similar, and can suffer from the same problems, although photos are used instead of drawings.

Stealomatics are like moving mood boards, with snippets 'stolen' from other ads, and are very useful for conveying an emotion or a mood, particularly with a good music track. However, respondents can get too locked into executional details and will suspect that the ad is going to be derivative.

Storyboards can be exposed frame by frame in a flip chart, with a narrative tape or a backing track if desired, which requires some coordination.

Key frames can be quite adequate for a simple story, and can be used with a narrative tape, or a script that is read out. A more open-ended alternative is to give respondents the script and some descriptions, and let them tell the interviewer how they visualised the ad. Narrative tapes work well for respondents who favour an auditory modality for information processing, but others may need to be encouraged to visualise the scenes being described.

There is no approved list of stimulus material. Advertising and design agencies have their own favourite types, but it is possible to invent completely new ones, for example using a puppet theatre, real actors, or getting respondents to act it themselves. Book 6 gives a fuller description of advertising stimulus material and the issues involved in working with it.

### Choosing and Developing Stimulus Material

This section refers specifically to the last role for stimulus material – to represent an idea, a product, a commercial, which does not yet exist. The two underlying principles in deciding what type of material to use are:

> choosing something that recreates or reflects the key elements as closely as possible – and which can communicate well to respondents; and

> choosing something that will enable the researcher to find out how and why it will be effective – will fulfil its intended role.

There is a distinction between the material and the underlying idea, and respondents may reject the material for any number of reasons without necessarily rejecting the essence of the idea it represents.

The arena of advertising research is fraught with misunderstanding because researchers are often asked to make a judgement about whether something will 'work' (evoke the desired response), without knowing how it is supposed to 'work', or what precisely the desired response is. The starting point is to understand the intentions of the client, and the rationale behind the particular expression of the idea that has been chosen for the research. This will involve asking many questions, including some of the following.

- What job is it (the advertising/packaging etc.) trying to do?
- Who is it talking to – and why have they been chosen?
- What should respondents think and/or feel when they see it?
- How is it supposed to do that?
- What parts are rational, and what emotional communication is there?
- What will they say or do if it works? (What exactly will the researcher be able to see or hear to know that it works?)
- What is strategy and what is execution?

The 'method' by which it is to 'work' could include: education (factual or emotional), endorsement, sharing (a joke, or a value system), identification, humour (feelgood or entertainment), fantasy or wish fulfilment, warmth and reassurance, idealisation or symbolism, or any combination of these!

If possible, the best way to present the idea is to use all the senses, as then people who are visual, auditory, or kinaesthetic in their information processing will stand an equal chance of appreciating it.

So, for example, if consumers will need to identify with the characters in the advertising, the stimulus material will have to help them do that – perhaps through pictures and descriptions of what they are like. If there is a joke to be conveyed, then timing and narration might be important, and it might be better to use a pre-recorded tape rather than rely on the researcher's sense of comedy. If the idea is to create warmth and luxury, music, warm colours and rich textures might convey this best. Some concepts are very hard to convey by a drawing alone. The shine and fullness of glossy hair, the sensual thick texture of cream pouring – if these are key to the appreciation of the idea, it might be necessary to have additional photos, fabrics, textures and so on.

### Using Stimulus Material

Again, this section refers to working with the most difficult type of stimulus material; that which represents new concepts and ideas rather than existing ones.

One of the most common mistakes made by novice researchers is to confuse the strategy (the underlying idea) with the execution (its form as stimulus). Respondents can be very critical in groups, and they will often say they don't like the people, they don't like the music, and they don't like the story. The young researcher concludes they don't like the ad, so it won't work. Yet the basic strategy of the ad may be correct – it will say what is needed about the brand. It will just need careful casting, new music and a more interesting scenario.

Interviewers have to explain patiently that this material cannot show exactly what it would be like, and that it is possible to change elements of it. It helps to have stimulus material that is open-ended, or can be backed up by open-ended techniques such as a picture sort. If it is the wrong sort of living room, can they please find a picture that approximates to the right sort of living room? In the dialogue between client, advertising or design agency and research company, stimulus material can play a very political role, its ultimate form reflecting some of the power struggles that have taken place in its development. At the debrief the researcher steps back into this political situation, and is most strongly placed if he or she can assess how the stimulus material worked, what it communicated, how it was adapted or improved and what this means in terms of the project.

Another issue that has to be taken into account is the distinction between rational and emotional communication. Since a discussion is mainly a verbal (left brain) process, it tends to be analytical (see Chapter 4 on brain hemisphere differentiation). Often advertising ideas have a holistic, emotional (right brain) component, which can be destroyed through verbal analysis. The key to this is to switch respondents into right brain processing first, maybe by doing a projective technique, or even more simply by using music or examples of other ads that work in an emotional, holistic manner. Respondents can then experience it as intended before putting their feelings into words, which gives an entirely different result.

When working with multi-sensory stimulus material, it is useful to notice which channels convey what type of information. For example, the pictures can tell the story, the voiceover gives the rational proposition and the music gives an emotional tone. In researching direct mail, the order of opening the pack and looking at the pieces is important, so it will be useful to produce a mock up and watch how people handle it.

The degree of realism and the quality of finish of the material will depend on how much the quality of the execution is going to be an important factor in the response to the finished product. If it is important that something should look up-market, stimulus material that is glossy and well-finished will convey this better than a rough drawing.

## PROJECTIVE AND ENABLING TECHNIQUES

### *Their Role and Importance*

It is a defining feature of qualitative market research that it explores motivations, desires and needs (as well as behaviour), and it is accepted that not all aspects of these will be accessible to conscious awareness.

Researchers may simply accept the above as an implicit part of their world-view, or may subscribe to one or more of a range of theories, including the psychoanalytic unconscious, the more positive Humanistic version of the unconscious; neuropsychological theories about selection and processing out of conscious awareness; and/or a cultural analysis view, where common cultural assumptions are 'unconscious' because they are invisible. These theories work on different levels so it is possible to accept aspects of all of them without contradiction. Whatever the theory, researchers need practical means of accessing this material, and projective and enabling techniques are an important way of doing so.

The category of projective and enabling techniques includes methods such as word association, analogies, personification, collages, guided visualisation, role play, self-scripts and job references. In all these the brand or the organisation being studied is the central theme of the technique. They are called 'projective' techniques because some of the original ones were based on the psychoanalytic concept of projection, in which a disowned aspect of the self is projected outwards onto another person or organisation. The term 'enabling' was added to clarify that some techniques facilitated expression through mechanisms other than projection. New techniques are constantly being developed, some of which are adaptations from work-shops and training sessions. Amongst others, management trainers have developed a large repertoire of approaches for increasing self- and group awareness, some of which adapt well into 'projectives'. See, for example, the *Gamesters' Handbook* by Brandes and Phillips (1979).

While projective and enabling techniques are not the only route to uncovering the 'invisible mechanics of consumption', qualitative market researchers find them effective in doing so. They do this by:

- Giving access to other forms of processing information. Instead of thinking analytically in words, respondents can process information more holistically in pictures, or through the auditory or kinaesthetic channels. (Most of the insights from these processes are eventually put into words, since they are common currency for research reporting.)
- Encouraging the sharing of private and socially unacceptable thoughts and feelings, by making it safe to talk about them and 'projecting' them outwards, so they do not have to be personally owned.
- Helping overcome embarrassment and inhibitions, and helping respondents express themselves by giving them time to reflect, and the tools to do so. Even where feelings are fully available to conscious awareness, these techniques can make them clearer, better articulated and more meaningful.
- Stimulating the right brain activities of fantasy, imagination, creativity, metaphor and synthesis. This avoids over-reliance on the left brain, verbal-analytical style that standard interviewing processes tend to encourage.
- Giving insight into ways of thinking and processing as well as the contents of those thoughts.
- Interrupting normal ways of thinking to give a view of what is normally implicit, trivial, taken-for-granted.
- Giving respondents ways of focusing on a narrow subject that keeps them engaged and motivated.

The role of projectives overlaps with that of stimulus material as a tool for stimulating discussion, but the key difference is that with projectives the respondent provides the content.

The benefits to the researcher include greater depth, colour and nuance; an understanding of complex and irrational processes, a meaningful way of working with abstract constructs such as a brand or an organisational culture, fine discriminations between outwardly similar brands, products or services, and being able to evaluate emotional and holistic propositions in the way in which they were intended to be received. There are process benefits as well – the group bonds together and shares responsibility for understanding and problem-solving. Techniques can be introduced to change the energy of a group, to lighten up or become deeper, or to halt difficult dynamics by doing an individual or paired exercise.

It should be emphasised that the techniques are a means to an end, not an end in themselves. The 'result' of the technique is not the finding, but the implications of it. Clients often like to know what the techniques have brought to light, and can become very engaged with the idea that their organisation or product can be compared to a St Bernard dog, for example. However, this can be misinterpreted unless the interviewer has analysed exactly what this means in practice – is it that the organisation commands tenacious loyalty, or is it only adapted for a limited range of circumstances?

### Working at Different Levels

In discussing projective and enabling techniques in the past, writers have presented diagrams of 'layers of consciousness', to describe what parts of the psyche the different techniques access. Lannon and Cooper (1983), Valentine and Evans (1993) and Branthwaite (1995) between them describe a number of models. Figure 8.2 (opposite) shows a simplified summary of some of the key features of these models.

### Different Types of Technique

There is no single comprehensive theory that covers the rationales for all the techniques that are used, nor is there a simple method for classifying the techniques. Trying to group them together is like herding cats, as several of them could be in more than one group simultaneously.

In Book 1, Mike Imms and Gill Ereaut use a variant of the Johari Window to explain four quadrants that cover the uses of projective and enabling techniques:

**Conscious factors:** Public and spoken – the things people are aware of, and will say (to others)

**Private feelings:** Private but suppressed – the things people are aware of but won't say to others

**Intuitive associations:** Potentially public but unspoken because there is no vocabulary

**Unconscious factors:** Private and repressed – unknown both to the conscious self and to others

This adaptation of the Johari Window can be used as a way of grouping projectives, although some projectives fit into more than one category, and a few refuse to be classified altogether. Figure 8.3 (p. 130) shows an approximation of how this might look.

Given that some of the techniques can also be specifically used to address the social and the cultural, probably the most inclusive model is Alan Branthwaite's (1995) Domains of Influence on Consumer Actions. (The model is reproduced in Chapter 9 as part of a discussion on methodologies.) He distinguishes the Personal (the individual's inner experience) from the Rational, which is the individual's take from external social and cultural influences, and consists of internalised knowledge, beliefs, perceptions, including advertising and marketing claims. These are both

| Layer | Description | Method of access/role of projectives | Respondent barriers |
|---|---|---|---|
| Outer: public rational | Spontaneous and reasoned information easily accessible to consciousness | Direct questions and enabling techniques to enable more evocative descriptions and explanations | 'I'm not creative/good at expressing myself' |
| Private: social pressures | Accessible to consciousness, but kept private by mechanisms such as stereotyping, impression management, roles and games | Creating a 'safe' trusting, accepting and non-judgemental environment for expression, using projection and gentle challenging | 'If I tell you, you won't like me' |
| Intuitive associations | Things people don't know they know | Cues to open up associations Provide a visual or verbal vocabulary Ways of noticing and verbalising | 'It's nothing important/I can't express it.' |
| Symbolic/ cultural | Symbols and icons work because they are not consciously analysed | Symbolic material emerges through imaginative tasks. It is thematic, tonal and atmospheric. Cultural values emerge through analysis of assumptions | 'I don't believe in it/I don't want to know' |
| Unconscious: repressed thoughts, feelings and desires | Material that troubles the integrity of the Ego | Unlikely to emerge – not ethical or useful to work with; needs a skilled therapeutic setting | |

FIGURE 8.2    ***Working at different levels: Summary of the key features of layers of consciousness models***

| Quadrant | Task of projectives | Techniques |
|---|---|---|
| Conscious factors | More descriptive, lateral and imaginative | Association Analogy Personification Imagination Bubble drawing, Mapping |
| Private feelings | Give permission to reveal, acceptance | Sentence completion Bubble drawing Personification Collage School report Self-scripts |
| Intuitive associations | Dig deeper and make revelation safe and non-judgemental | Self-scripts Storytelling, Laddering Role play Collage Personification Guided imagery |
| Unconscious factors | Express the inaccessible Glimpse the symbolic, tonal and atmospheric | Mapping Psychodrawing Role play Modelling Collage Guided imagery |

FIGURE 8.3  *Grouping of projective techniques*

private or internal. In the public or external dimension are the Social (pressures and expectations, needs for identity and conformity) and the Cultural (collective wisdom, accepted practices, rules and obligations, myths and symbols).

In Figure 8.4 Branthwaite offers a grouping of techniques based on their usefulness in accessing these different domains, especially in a cross-cultural context. He puts some techniques in more than one domain, and limits himself to the most widely used ones, which achieves some consistency.

However, Branthwaite's model still mainly deals with the core techniques that usually come under the label of projectives, whereas in practice interviewers and moderators use a wider range of techniques, sometimes also called enabling, elicitation or creative techniques.

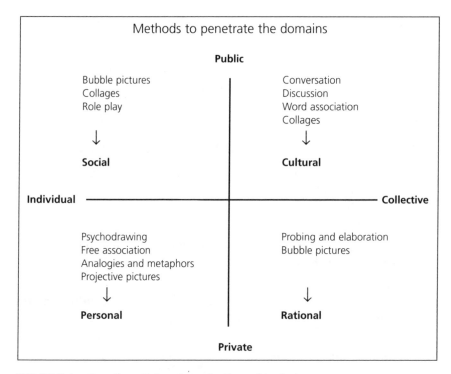

FIGURE 8.4    ***Branthwaite's categorisation of techniques***
**(Branthwaite, 1995 p. 89; reproduced with permission)**

Book 5 on developing brands with qualitative research offers detailed descriptions of some of these techniques and more. (Such techniques are particularly appropriate for work with brands.) Chandler and Owen (Book 5) classify them into general research techniques, those for needs research, brand language techniques, brand relationship techniques and techniques to identify meaning sets.

A full model would have to include several independent dimensions:

- The public (what the consumer will say), vs. the private (what the consumer won't normally say).
- Conscious awareness – what is known or accessible to consciousness, what can be made accessible, and what is very unlikely to be accessible.
- The individual, the social and the cultural or collective.
- Verbal vs. visual, vs. kinaesthetic or embodied.
- The rational, the intuitive and the emotional.
- That which has been processed (already formed opinions and attitudes) vs. that which is yet to be processed in conscious awareness (spontaneous).

## *Brief Descriptions of Some Enabling and Projective Techniques*

The techniques may be better described and categorised by being labelled more precisely, even though in practice researchers call them 'projectives', 'games' or 'tasks'. These categories include:

- **Enabling:** for an imagination warm-up, a move into right brain processes
- **Elicitation:** enabling insights into the subject being researched by:

  o Translation: from one modality to another, or from one conceptual structure to another
  o Association
  o Completion

- **Projective:** giving insight into the respondent and their motivations
- **Intrusive:** to break through the surface account:

  o Reactive (do rather than say)
  o Disruptive: disrupt the existing rules of the taken-for-granted world in order to see what they are

- **Structuring**
- **Exploratory and creative**.

**Enabling** techniques are used as a precursor to using one of the others. Success with techniques relies on having respondents in the right frame of mind; feeling imaginative, creative, playful (in Transactional Analysis terms, in Child mode). Enabling techniques are used to manage the transition from the analytical Adult (in TA) to Child, and to persuade respondents that they do have the ability to be imaginative. Often respondents underplay their creative potential, having been educated to believe that 'knowing things' is far more valuable than 'making things up'. An example of an enabling technique would be for the interviewer to read a highly descriptive passage, alluding to all the senses, and ask respondents to imagine the scenario. They discover they can imagine a glass of blue water hanging upside down in mid-air, or that their mouths start watering as they are about to bite into an imaginary lemon. Another technique is to play a piece of music and discuss the feelings and visual images it inspires. It is also possible to use one of the simpler techniques such as word association as a warm-up for a longer one.

**Elicitation** techniques are sometimes also called enabling, because they enable the respondents to talk about the subject with greater fluency than would be possible otherwise. Some of them ask the respondent to translate the subject into a different frame of reference: Analogies and Metaphors (e.g. if this were an animal, what would it be?) or Personification (imagining the brand as a person, describing its characteristics and life style). Personification can be extended into a Brand Party, a description of how all the competitive brands would behave at a party – who would be dancing wildly, who would be sitting in the kitchen and who would be staring out of the window hoping their car wasn't going to be stolen. (There are examples of some of these techniques being used in a therapeutic setting; Virginia Satir used the idea of a Parts Party, in which all the sub-personalities got together to sort out their differences.) Another variation is the School Report, in which the respondent in the role of teacher assesses the strengths, weaknesses and 'must try harder' of the brand. The Job Reference is very similar, while the Obituary is useful with brands that receive a lot of negative criticism, as obituaries tend to focus on positive achievements. Picture Sorts or Collages, which can be ready-made or picked out by respondents (which is better, especially if they are instructed not to think while doing it, but choose the pictures intuitively and rationalise later), are a very powerful technique. Since 'each picture says a thousand words', they give new and creative insights into brands and organisations, discriminate well between outwardly similar brands, and often give insights into personal motivations and cultural norms into the bargain. This technique can be put into many categories.

Word Association was used by the earliest psychologists to trace patterns of associations between concepts, and is still used nowadays, sometimes in combination with a sorting or mapping technique to cluster the words into higher order meanings. Completion techniques start with an aspect of the brand or organisation, and then invite the respondent to go further in imagination. At a simple level, there is Sentence Completion, but it also works with Storytelling (elaborating a story from a simple scenario related to the brand), and Guided Imagery (or Visualisation) in which the respondents imagine a room, building, or planet entirely devoted to that brand and suffused with its characteristics, and then share the descriptions with each other.

**Projective** techniques in the pure sense are based on the psychological mechanism of projecting onto others disowned parts of the self. The classic clinical technique in the 1950s and 1960s was the Rorschach Ink Blot Test. People were given a series of ink blots to look at and had to describe the shapes and patterns they saw in them. Psychologists then scored these and assessments were made – a feature of projectives that researchers avoid. These techinques can work in a very light way, as with Bubble drawings – cartoons in which the speech and thought bubbles have to be filled in by respondents. These can be elaborated into dialogues between consumers and brands, or even between brands themselves. Any socially undesirable responses are then seen as coming from the people in the cartoons rather than from respondents themselves.

Creating a Typical User involves large elements of projection, as well as highlighting cultural judgements and expectations about 'the type of person' who uses such a product. In Self-scripts, respondents write about their own behaviour in the third person, which frees them from some self-censorship, while the act of stepping outside and reflecting on behaviour reveals embedded thoughts and feelings. Clay Modelling and Psychodrawing are versions of a projective technique. They start by getting respondents to access a feeling related to the subject, one that is hard to verbalise. Respondents are then instructed to allow their hand to make shapes and colours (Psychodrawing) or a three-dimensional model of the feeling (Modelling). In this manner, the feeling is projected outwards, and the drawing or model can be examined in order to verbalise some of the aspects of the feeling. Note that projection makes it safer to talk about the feeling; it is no longer part of the respondent but an external object – which, however, should still be treated respectfully.

Chandler and Owen (Book 5) describe **Intrusive** techniques. They provide a stimulus or trigger revealing some of the unconscious processing that has gone into creating the meaning structure of the brand. They have two particularly interesting sub-categories. **Reactive** techniques are designed to force consumers to do rather than say – for example, Advertising Graffiti, in which consumers are encouraged to doodle all over advertising and communications material, before being invited to comment on these. They also describe **disruptive** techniques, in which the task is to disrupt or confront the existing rules of the everyday world. Product Deprivation – not being allowed to use the product for a period of time – and Product Saturation – being given several different products to use simultaneously – reveal a lot of responses that would normally be considered too trivial and obvious to be articulated.

**Structuring** techniques are a necessary counterpoint to all the stimulating and creative techniques, providing some sense of order and insight into the consumer's internal logic and priorities. One of the most common is brand or product mapping, in which respondents are instructed to 'group together all the ones that go together', and then to explain the clusters they form. This can be developed into more sophisticated or prompted forms and has the added advantage of revealing respondents' vocabulary. A cross between mapping and personification is Brand Families, where it is important to expose the relationships between products or parts of an organisation. Children can do simple sorting tasks with product attributes written on cards.

Two techniques have been borrowed from Personal Construct Psychology, both of which are designed to work in depth interviews rather than in groups. One is the Repertory Grid, sometimes known as the Kelly Grid – a way of eliciting the key dimensions by which a person relates to the world, and then rating people, brands, or organisations on those dimensions. More often used, and especially favoured in the USA and Germany, is Laddering, or Means End Analysis. This starts with dimensions or attributes, and seeks to discover higher order constructs by asking the consumer 'why is it important to you that you have (naming the attribute)?' Computer programs have been developed to process the individual responses into clusters of typologies, and some companies specialise in doing large projects of specialist laddering interviews.

**Exploratory and creative** techniques sometimes come under the banner of projectives, since many of the techniques described above are creative, and can be slightly adjusted to provide 'what if' scenarios. A technique borrowed from NLP, Timelines, invites respondents to draw or visualise the history of a brand or organisation, and then to project into the future by extending the timeline. Collages can work as well for exploring ideas that are not fully formed, as for existing products or services. As researchers become more involved in some of their clients' internal processes, they may organise brainstorming sessions or joint workshops. Within this frame of reference there are hundreds of techniques that are well documented in resources for creative consultants and workshop leaders. Some of these ideas can be expected to be adapted for consumer groups as they become better known.

### Using and Interpreting Projective Techniques

There is a tendency to make projective techniques safe and light by referring to them as 'games'. While this is sometimes useful, it does not make for informed choice. Best practice is to obtain some understanding of the theory behind the use of the main techniques, and to make a conscious decision about which ones are useful and comfortable for the interviewer to work with. It is axiomatic that the interviewer or moderator should only use techniques that he or she would be comfortable doing; hence it is important that moderators try out techniques for themselves in training.

It is possible to use some of the techniques at a moment's notice and with no preparation. Word association, personification and mapping need only the presence of some packs or logos, and often work with a minimum of introduction. However, there are some projects where the use of projectives is central, and some of the more involved techniques will be used. For these projects, preparation is essential:

- Preparation of the appropriate materials.
- Making enough time for the technique, the interpretation and the subsequent discussion in the topic guide.
- Preparing respondents for the idea that they will be doing more than talking from the earliest stage. In the introduction, moderators can describe the research task in terms of 'looking at many different aspects of the product in many different ways', which will stop respondents from being so surprised when the moderator suggests a drawing or a collage. Other moderators will have crayons available from the start and encourage respondents to write their names in crayon or to doodle all the way through.
- The technique needs to be introduced at the appropriate stage of group development. While mapping can be used early on and helps group development, many of the other techniques need to be used

once trust has been built up and the group is nearing or is at the performing stage.

- Moderators should use techniques they are comfortable with, otherwise respondents will sense their unease.
- Introducing the techniques is part of the art of using them. Some can be introduced as a game, some as 'another way of looking at things'. It may help to acknowledge that some respondents find them a little odd, or to demonstrate them if this can be done without prejudicing the result. The tone of voice of the introduction is also important; it needs to be confident and encouraging, and playful if appropriate. However, respondents should not feel forced to take part, and the moderator has to be equally convincing that it is perfectly all right if some people sit this out. They can be brought into the discussion that ensues after the issues have been uncovered. Cordwell and Gabbot (1999) offer a salutary reminder that creating the right atmosphere for projectives is essential to obtaining any value from them.
- Respondents quickly come to understand the idea, and subsequent techniques need less introduction than the first one. However, they should be paced well to avoid creative burnout.
- In the case of techniques that require some interpretation, this should always come from the respondent him or herself. This enables the moderator to maintain a non-judgemental stance, involves respondents and allows self-censoring of any material the respondent does not want to disclose. Best practice is to ask respondents for comments on the exercise and what they learnt from it, and to use these to stimulate further discussion within the group.
- For completely mysterious reasons, some techniques fail to work with some groups of people, even if preparation has been thorough. This has to be accepted as an occupational hazard, and should not give rise to self-blame. Most moderators have an entire toolbox of techniques, and if one doesn't work, they will simply go on to another.

## CONCLUSION

There are many similarities between stimulus material and projective techniques. Stimulus material can often become the basis of a projective – packs are used for mapping and personification, a frame from a storyboard can become the starting point for storytelling and so on. A large set of tear sheets from magazines not only works for collages, but can also be used on the spot to augment visual stimulus material that is misleading or distracting. Some projects need extensive use of stimulus material and/or projective techniques; others include some usage because of the benefits for the interviewing process. These benefits include respondent involvement, richness, colour and nuance in the findings, ways of working with very abstract concepts, the ability to work with or alter group processes, and above all, the ability to fulfil the client brief for insight and understanding of the 'invisible mechanics of consumption' within the time and budgetary constraints.

**KEY POINTS**

- Qualitative market researchers use stimulus material to focus and deepen the interviewing process. Stimulus material includes anything from logos, pack designs, products, photographs and videos to proposed designs for places, products or systems, ideas for commercials and other forms of communication.
- Stimulus material is used to involve respondents before and during the research, speed up group formation, enable the respondents to say more about the subject and to present new ideas in a concrete form in order to be able to discuss them. It helps to develop hypotheses, and to ground the research in a representation of reality. It acts as a cue to trigger stored associations and emotions, which have not yet been processed consciously.
- Stimulus material has process benefits. It often helps a group to bond faster. Respondents forget their own anxieties as they become involved in the research issues. It can be used to change patterns of communication within a group and help with respondents who are not contributing well.
- The vast range of possibilities for stimulus material causes problems for researchers and clients alike when deciding what to use. Material has to be introduced and handled carefully, as it has the potential to mislead.
- Projective and enabling techniques also keep respondents engaged with the research issues and enable them to say more. These techniques help respondents articulate more creatively what they are aware of, and shed light on what was previously the intuitive and inexpressible. They encourage the sharing of private and unacceptable thoughts, uncovering hidden emotions, as well as bringing to light the cultural codes that frame behaviour. They can illuminate how people think as well as what they are thinking. Their role overlaps with that of stimulus material, but they are mostly structured so that the consumer provides the content.
- The techniques produce interesting descriptions, drawings, collages, models etc., but their true value lies in the interpretations and insights they bring. Qualitative researchers ask respondents to interpret their own work and use the new insights to stimulate further discussion.
- The benefits to the researcher include greater depth, colour and nuance; an understanding of complex and irrational processes, a meaningful way of working with abstract constructs such as a brand

or an organisational culture, fine discriminations between outwardly similar brands, products or services, and being able to evaluate emotional and holistic propositions in the way in which they were intended to be received.

- There is a wide range of techniques that have overlapping functions, but it is possible to make some approximate groupings. There is endless potential to develop these techniques, but certain principles about applying them have to be borne in mind.
- Used well, stimulus material and projective techniques hugely increase the amount of richness and depth that can be obtained from the interviewing process, and enable commercial researchers to meet their objectives within budgetary and timing requirements.

# 'Informed Eclecticism': Choosing and Using Interviewing Approaches

**Qualitative market researchers can choose from a large range of options for interviewing and moderating approaches. Much research is ad hoc, and proposals are based, at least in part, on the researcher's tacit knowledge and intuition. This allows for some creativity in designing methodologies, but the experience takes time for novice researchers to acquire, and may mean some possibilities are neglected.**

**It has been said that research needs a new paradigm for the twenty-first century and qualitative market research is well placed to evolve towards this vision of 'informed eclecticism'. The challenge is to make connections between the theories that are involved in this vision and their manifestation at the interfaces of interviewing.**

**Book 1 gives a detailed description of the factors involved in project design and management; this chapter explores possibilities for adopting a more informed and integrated approach to devising interviewing strategies.**

Qualitative market researchers work with the client, the objectives, the timing and the budget to create the most appropriate methodology, implicitly borrowing from several different theories in the process. There are broad principles for project design, but the process may not be formally defined – it is a mixture of education, experience and intuition. The researcher who puts together a proposal and writes an outline topic guide has to be sure it will deliver. How is it done? How to choose from the endless possibilities of combinations of methodologies, moderator roles, questioning styles, projective and enabling techniques, and types of stimulus material? The lack of attachment to theory has to date encouraged fluidity, flexibility and willingness to experiment. But it has also meant that potentially useful ideas and techniques are not considered, and the ones that are used are not exploited to the full. The time is coming to move from unconscious competence to conscious competence. In a competitive and changing environment, conscious and deliberate use of theory can be a benefit. Qualitative market researchers have always been eclectic; now they need to be more informed.

Spackman, Barker and Nancarrow (2000) discuss their view of a new paradigm for the market research industry (both qualitative and quantitative) and describe it as 'informed eclecticism'. The characteristics of this paradigm include:

- Drawing people and ideas from disciplines outside of research to provide different perspectives.
- Adopting a bricolage approach, which is 'the bringing together of those specialisms to form a coherent and exciting whole which will always be greater than the sum of its parts' (2000: 101).
- Developing working relationships between commercial researchers and academics/theoreticians, and making more specific use of theory, including mini-theories.
- Promoting staff development and shared learning through 'non-competitive client alliances'.
- Developing a risk culture, which is 'more than just an entrepreneurial empathy; it is also about creating a spirit of adventure and inspiration ...' (2000: 101).
- Communicating research insights effectively.

Qualitative market research is best placed to develop this paradigm, with many signs of interest in bricolage, anthropology, semiotics, cultural analysis and a historical openness to methodological pluralism. Few qualitative market researchers maintain that one favoured approach can explain all the complex systems they encounter; different models are useful for developing insights and approaches that relate to specific situations.

Spackman, Barker and Nancarrow also identify a major barrier to the development of informed eclecticism, which this chapter can start to address:

> How, at a project level, can researchers identify, choose and use competing theories, models, metaphors? (2000: 102)

The subject is clearly larger than qualitative interviewing; it has to include non-interviewing methodologies and analysis procedures. Nevertheless, it also includes the question:

> How do researchers choose the most appropriate interviewing setting, style and approach, from the vast range of possible options?

It is not appropriate to be prescriptive; but it may be helpful to outline a framework that supports the processes. The development of an interviewing strategy requires interlocking decisions at a number of levels:

TABLE 9.1 *Suiting the interviewing style to the research task*

| Research task | Researcher's mode/questioning style |
| --- | --- |
| Describing a current situation | Journalist/psychologist/anthropologist |
| Theory-building | Academic/hermeneutic |
| Exploring or generating new possibilities | Inventor, enabler |
| Developing strategic or creative options | Strategist |
| Assessing potential reactions | Reality modeller |
| Diagnosing/analysing a situation or brand | Detective, analyst |
| Evaluating a situation or intervention | Scientist, investigator |

1   An understanding of the character and nature of the research project, which will suggest an appropriate strategic approach.
2   A choice about which domains of influence on respondent actions (and underlying theoretical models) can most usefully be explored to answer the objectives.
3   Therefore identifying which techniques will most effectively help with that exploration.

These three levels are now considered in turn.

## THE CHARACTER AND NATURE OF THE RESEARCH AND THE STRATEGIC APPROACH

Chapter 2 outlines the main types of project carried out by qualitative market researchers, which are: screening, exploration, strategic development, diagnostic assessment, creative development and evaluation. These can be thought of as stages in a cycle of development. Sometimes projects involve two or three of these stages simultaneously, as when a client wants an update on background information, help in choosing a new packaging design, and an evaluation of recent advertising. Each of these stages or tasks demands a different approach to designing the interviews and the topic guides, and the moderator needs to be in the appropriate mode to work with the respondents (see Table 9.1).

At this stage some elements of the research approach will be clear – how broad, how creative, how open-ended or constrained, to what extent actual or reported behaviour is required, and so on.

Assessing the research task and the interviewing mode helps to answer some of the issues about 'how', but there is a need to define 'what' is going to be explored in order to answer the research issues. A broad structure for looking at this issue is usefully provided by Branthwaite's diagram of 'Domains of Influence on Consumer Actions' (see Figure 9.1). The usefulness of exploring and probing each domain can be assessed when putting together the proposal. Since interviewers may be researching

| | Public/external | |
|---|---|---|
| **Social** | | **Cultural** |
| Social/family pressures and expectations<br>Compromise and conformity<br>Identity and distinctiveness | | Myths, folklore and language<br>Collective wisdom<br>Accepted practices<br>Rules and obligations<br>Volues, symbols and icons |
| **Individual** ———————————————— | | ———————— **Collective** |
| **Personal** | | **Rational** |
| Individual experience<br>Feeling and emotions<br>Private associations<br><br>Intuitive images<br><br>Unconscious connections | | Internalised knowledge, facts<br>Shared beliefs and perceptions<br>(Social) justification and rationalisation<br>Perceived advertising and marketing claims |
| | Private/internal | |

FIGURE 9.1 *Domains of influence on consumer actions* (Branthwaite, 1995 p. 88; reproduced with permission)

people who are not in a consumer role, it can perhaps be retitled 'Domains of Influence on People's Actions', as it seems to have broad applications.

## DOMAINS OF INFLUENCE AND THEORETICAL MODELS

The key dimensions on which these domains are structured are individual and collective, and public/external vs. private/internal. These quadrants represent all the main factors that might influence actions. Bearing in mind the overall purpose and nature of the research, the researcher has to decide to what extent it will be useful

- to delve into the personal – individual experience, feelings, motivations, associations;
- to understand belief systems, shared perceptions, decision-making processes and behaviour;
- to look at the influence of external factors in building individual and social identity, and the influences on individual brand relationships;
- to assess the influence of the social, media and cultural context in which all this happens – and that the respondent may not be aware of.

| | **Public/external** | |
|---|---|---|
| **Social** | | **Cultural** |
| Group dynamics | | Anthropological and cultural studies |
| Humanistic psychologies | | Semiotics |
| | | Transpersonal |
| Projectives | | Mythological |
| Social and family systems | | Theories of communication and media |

**Individual** ———————————————————————————————————— **Collective**

| **Personal** | | **Rational** |
|---|---|---|
| 'I' language | | Cognitive science |
| Introspective psychologies | | Behavioural approaches |
| Psychodynamics | | Decision-making processes |
| Stream of consciousness | | Theories about media and consumption |

| | **Private/internal** | |

FIGURE 9.2  *Domains of influence and theoretical models*

Other factors will affect the choice – particularly the use to which the research will be put, and the client's degree of interest in depth exploration and theory. 'Do people want coloured laptops?' as a research issue will not be as complex as 'How can we encourage people to keep trying to give up smoking?'

Each of the domains is served by a set of theories that relate partly or mainly to that realm and give the researcher a starting point both for choosing theoretical models and methodological options (see Figure 9.2). To give an example, the giving up smoking project might be tackled in any or all of the domains depending on the specific brief.

In the **personal** domain, it would be about the conscious and unconscious needs smoking is fulfilling and how those might be reassessed or met elsewhere. Such an interview would need the building of an individual and sensitive relationship with each respondent, and much time for introspection as well as techniques to aid insight. The psychodynamic tradition would provide a choice of theoretical models that might be helpful in conceptualising the findings.

The **rational** domain would focus on the triggers that encourage smoking, the behaviours and situations that cause relapses, information and beliefs people have about smoking and how that information is evaluated and integrated into their belief systems. Such a project might include behavioural tasks, evaluations of advertising communications, and the messages sent by various brands. Both Cognitive Therapy and Rational Emotive Therapy could be used as sources for adapting research interventions and understanding the relationships between information and behaviour.

The **social** domain would cover not only social situations for smoking, but also how the smoker believes she or he is perceived by others, and perceives other smokers. Making use of projectives, it would explore how the identity of the smoker is constructed and the relationship the smoker has with cigarettes in general and his or her brands in particular. Theories of group dynamics and the roles people play for others would be helpful.

The **cultural** domain might include aspects the smoker is not personally aware of – in what ways the culture signals it is cool to smoke, the ritual and mythical significance of smoking, emergent trends that devalue smoking and so on. Some of these may emerge from interviews; others may need studies that do not rely on the individual smoker as a source of information. The approach may be semiotic, anthropological, or based on a cultural analysis.

## CHOOSING INTERVIEWING TECHNIQUES AND STRATEGIES

The *how* of the research mode and the *what* of the domains of influence provide the *why* – the rationale for choosing specific interviewing techniques and strategies.

Questions about *who* and *where* are equally important. The complexities of these choices are described in detail in Book 1. They clearly impact on interviewing but have been set aside for the purpose of following the process from research objectives to interview questions and techniques.

The *how* and the *what* will influence decisions such as:

- The nature of the relationship needed with respondents.
- The need to ground the research with observation or reality testing.
- The depth of understanding of respondents' belief systems.
- The extent to which emotions need to be accessed and verbalised.
- The need to understand identities, value systems and relationships between people and/or services, organisations and brands.

The researcher therefore knows *why* it will be useful to adopt particular interviewing approaches. Figure 9.3 relates these decisions to techniques and strategies that have been mentioned or described in this volume.

| Research task | Key words and concepts | Skills, strategies and techniques |
|---|---|---|
| Building a working relationship with the respondent(s) | Rapport, power, responsibility, support, challenge, respect, trust, ethics | **Physical** – non-verbal communication, self-presentation, the structure of the research<br>**Verbal** – the introduction, explanations about the research, managing relationships and process issues<br>**Emotional** – reflecting the inner world of the respondent; respecting their boundaries |
| 'Grounding', establishing 'facts', behaviours, past history, where relevant | What? Where? When? Narratives, stories, perceptions, descriptions | Check facts using closed questions<br>Open-ended questions to elicit 'journalistic' narratives and descriptions<br>Diaries, observation, self-scripts, trials and tasks<br>Specific examples, reductions to sensory data – what did you see, hear, feel? |
| Understanding the respondents' belief systems and thought processes | Knowledge, judgements, schema<br>Implicit structures<br>Decision-making processes<br>Needs<br>Beliefs, personal and cultural values | Eliciting and clarifying explanations of behaviour, lists of reasons and influences, prioritising, associating, connecting, mapping, laddering, behaviour modification<br>Re-enacting decision-making processes<br>Challenging and disrupting |
| Eliciting respondents' own feelings and motivations | Emotions, non-rational influences,<br>desires, moods<br>Preferences<br>Comfort levels | Active listening and reflecting<br>Using mood boards and collages<br>Techniques to attach weight to factors<br>Psychodrawing |
| Eliciting feelings and impressions about brands and organisations | Impressions, perceptions, images<br>Tacit knowledge | Word associations and mind mapping<br>Collages and picture sorts<br>Guided imagery<br>Storytelling<br>Metaphors, and analogies<br>Reports and 'obituaries' |
| Establishing the respondent's role(s), identity and relationships in consumption | Attributions<br>Ownership of issues and responsibilities<br>Roles and sub-personalities<br>Need states<br>Relationships with brands | Listening to the language – does 'you' mean 'me', another person or generalised others?<br>Perceptions: How do you see yourself? How do others see you? How do you and others see the brand? What sort of people use the brand? How does the brand see you?<br>Bubble pictures, brand and user personification, brand families, brand parties, guided imagery, collages and picture sorts |

(continued)

| Research task | Key words and concepts | Skills, strategies and techniques |
|---|---|---|
| Modelling reality – reactions to proposals Behaviour change | How? If? When? Key concepts strategy and execution | Phased exposition Stimulus material, hypothetical questions Scenarios Observation, research tasks and feedback |
| Supporting creativity and emergent ideas | How else? What else? New Unusual | Reframing Creative thinking strategies and games Open-ended exploration Drawing |
| Understanding family, co-worker and peer relationships | Roles Interpersonal influence Social Cultural | Observation Family/peer interviews Hierarchies of influence Relationship mapping |
| Theory-building (for further use by the client) | Typologies Psychographics Hypotheses Commonalities Patterns Hermeneutics | Structuring the sample and method to test hypotheses Focusing on reasons for commonalities and differences *during* the research Enacting and testing processes |

FIGURE 9.3  *Strategies and techniques for qualitative research tasks*

## CONCLUSION

Identifying the process that leads from the research brief to the structure, style and techniques of the interview is difficult and complex. This description of the process is not entirely realistic; many researchers find that staying within the budget and using methodologies the client understands are also prime concerns. Nevertheless, if qualitative market researchers are to move from using a serendipitous mix of experience and intuition to having a broad, segmented and theoretically based set of techniques at their disposal, some formalisation of processes will be required. There will also be a need for a broader education for researchers – more than can be provided by coaching and a few seminars, for the researcher will have to be able to think equally fluently within a wide range of disciplines.

## KEY POINTS

- Qualitative market researchers work within a set of broad principles for project design, but there is a large element of intuition and experience involved in translating a set of research objectives into an interview or topic guide. However, the new paradigm for research suggests benefits can be gained from a conscious use of theory, within an approach described as 'informed eclecticism'.
- The new paradigm involves the use of people and theories from outside the traditional disciplines of qualitative research, adopting a bricolage approach, in which the whole will always be greater than the sum of its parts.
- It is difficult to conceptualise the connection between the research brief, the theories that may be used to inform the research, and the questions or techniques that are used in the interviewing situation. However, there is a broad framework for the series of interlocking decisions that are made in order to arrive at the interview process:

  o Understanding the character and nature of the research, which guides *how* it should be approached.

  o Choosing which 'domains of influence' should be investigated, which helps define the *what* of the research, as well as indicating which types of theory will be helpful for both methodology and context.

  o Using the *how* and the *what* to provide guidance for the *why* – why certain techniques and approaches in interviewing will be useful.

- To work within the new paradigm qualitative market researchers will not only have to form new working alliances with other specialists and clients, but also become more educated about the range of theories available to them and how they impact on the issues of research and interviewing.

# Bibliography

Boeree, G. (1998) ttp://www.ship.edu/~cgboeree/qualmethfour.html

Brandes, B. and Phillips, H. (1979) *Gamesters' Handbook*. London: Hutchinson.

Branthwaite, A. (1995) 'Standardisation through creative expression: projective techniques in international market research', *Canadian Journal of Marketing Research*, 14: pp. 87–93.

Carter, R. (2000) *Mapping the Mind*. London: Phoenix.

Catterall, M. (2000) 'Analysis and interpretation: academic and practitioner perspectives compared'. Paper given at AQR Seminar on Analysis and Interpretation, London, June 2000. St. Neots, Cambridgeshire: AQR.

Chandler, J. and Owen, M. (1989) 'Genesis to Revelations – the evolution of qualitative philosophy, *Proceedings of the Market Research Society Conference*. London: MRS. pp. 295–305.

Chandler, J. and Owen, M. (2002) *Developing Brands with Qualitative Market Research*. Book 5 in Gill Ereaut, Mike Imms and Martin Callingham (eds), *Qualitative Market Research* (7 volumes). London: Sage.

Checkman, D. (1989) 'Focus group research as theater: how it affects the players and their audience', *Marketing Research*, December 1989, pp. 33–40.

Chrzanowska, J. and Du Broff, N. (1988) 'Tuning into a better understanding: American dream or British nightmare?' Paper presented to the international section of the Market Research Society.

Collins, M. (1980) Interviewer variability: a review of the problem', *Journal of the Market Research Society*, 22 (2).

Cooper, P. (1990) 'Internationalisation of qualitative research'. ESOMAR Congress, Monte Carlo, special sessions.

Cooper, P. and Patterson, S. (2000) 'The trickster – creativity in modern advertising and branding', *Proceedings of the Market Research Society Conference*. London: MRS. pp. 105–19.

Cordwell, D. and Gabbott, D. (1999) 'Do we assume too much? A consumer's view of the qualitative experience', *Proceedings of the Market Research Society Conference*. London: MRS. pp. 223–32.

Cowley, J. (2000) 'Strategic qualitative focus group research – define and articulate our skills or we will be replaced by others', *International Journal of Market Research*, 42 (1): pp. 17–38.

Desai, P. (2002) *Methods Beyond Interviewing in Qualitative Market Research*. Book 3 in Gill Ereaut, Mike Imms and Martin Callingham (eds), *Qualitative Market Research* (7 volumes). London: Sage.

De Vault, M. (1990) 'Talking and listening from women's standpoint: feminist strategies for interviewing and analysis', *Social Problems*, 37(1):96–116.

Dolliver, R. (1995) 'Carl Rogers's personality theory and psychotherapy as a reflection of his life experience and personality', *Journal of Humanistic Psychology*, 35 (4): pp. 111–28.

Dixon, N.F. (1981) *Preconscious Processing*. New York: Wiley.

Fontana, A. and Frey, J.H. (1994) 'Interviewing: the art of science', in N. Denzin, and Y.S. Lincoln (eds), *Collecting and Interpreting Qualitative Materials*. Thousand Oaks: CA, Sage. pp. 47–78.

Forsyth, D.R. (1990) *Group Dynamics*. Pacific Grove, CA: Books/Cole.

Franzen, G. and Bouwman, M. (2001) *The Mental World of Brands: Mind, Memory and Brand Success*. Henley-on-Thames: World Advertising Research Centre.

Frey, J.H. and Fontana, A. (1993) 'The group interview in social research', in D.L. Morgan (ed.), *Successful Focus Groups*. Thousand Oaks, CA: Sage.

Goffman, E. (1971) *The Presentation of Self in Everyday Life*. Harmondsworth: Penguin.

Goleman, D. (1996) *Emotional Intelligence*. London: Bloomsbury.

Goodyear, M. (1996) 'Divided by a common language: diversity and deception in the world of global marketing', *Journal of the Market Research Society*, 38 (2): 105–22.

Gordon, W. (1997) *Is the Right Research Being Ill-used?* Henley-on-Thames: Admap.

Gordon, W. (1999) *Goodthinking: A Guide to Qualitative Research*. Henley-on-Thames: Admap.

Gordon, W. and Langmaid, R. (1988) *Qualitative Market Research: A Practitioner's and Buyer's Guide*. Aldershot: Gower.

Gordon, W. and Robson, S. (1982) 'Respondent through the Looking Glass: towards a better understanding of the qualitative interviewing process', *Proceedings of the Market Research Society Conference*. London: MRS. pp. 455–73.

Greenfield, Susan (2000) *The Private Life of the Brain*. London: Allen Lane/Penguin.

Hayes, N. (1994) *Teach Yourself Psychology*. London: Hodder Headline.

Hayward, W. and Rose, J. (1990) '"We'll meet again ..." Repeat attendance at group discussions – does it matter?', *Proceedings of the Market Research Society Conference*. London: MRS. pp. 177–92.

Heath, R. (1999) 'Just popping down to the shops for a packet of image statements', *Proceedings of the Market Research Society Conference*. London: MRS. pp. 145–57.

Heath, R. (2001) 'Low involvement processing'. Paper for Stretch Zone Seminar.

Hecker, S. (1981) 'A brain hemisphere orientation towards concept testing', *Journal of Advertising Research*, 21 (4): pp. 56–60.

Hutchby, I. and Wooffitt, R. (1998) *Conversation Analysis*. Cambridge: Polity Press.

Imms, M. (1999) 'A reassessment of the roots and theoretical basis of qualitative market research in the UK', *Proceedings of the Market Research Society Conference*. London: MRS. pp. 203–27.

Imms, M. and Ereaut, G. (2002) *An Introduction to Qualitative Market Research*. Book 1 in Gill Ereaut, Mike Imms and Martin Callingham (eds), *Qualitative Market Research* (7 volumes). London: Sage.

Krueger, R. (1998) 'Developing questions for focus groups', in *The Focus Group Kit*. London: Sage.

Lannon, J. and Cooper, P. (1983) 'Humanistic advertising: a holistic cultural perspective', *International Journal of Advertising*, 2 (3): 195–213.

Market Research Society R&D Sub-Committee on Qualitative Research (1979) 'Qualitative research: a summary of the concepts involved', *Journal of the Market Research Society*, 21 (2): 107–24.

Maslow, A.H. (1968) *Toward a Psychology of Being*. New York: Van Nostrand Reinhold.

Masson, J. (1990) *Against Therapy*. London: Fontana.

McCracken, G. (1988) *The Long Interview*. Qualitative Research Methods Series 13. London: Sage.

Mead, G.M. (1934) *Mind, Self and Society*. Chicago: University of Chicago Press.

Mearns, D. and Thorne, B. (1988) *Person-Centered Counselling in Action*. London: Sage.

Morgan, D.L. (ed.) (1993) *Successful Focus Groups*. Thousand Oaks, CA: Sage.

Noll, R. (1996) *The Jung Cult*. London: Fontana.

O'Connor, J. and McDermott, I. (1996) *Principles of NLP*. London: Thorsons.

Packard, V. (1957) *The Hidden Persuaders*. Harmondsworth: Penguin.

Parkin, A. (1999) *Memory: A Guide for Professionals*. Chichester: Wiley.

Pawle, J. (2000) 'A new view of global brand personality for the Millennium', *Proceedings of the Market Research Society Conference*. London: MRS. pp. 279–91.

Perrin, S. and Spencer, C. (1980) 'The Asch effect – a child of its time', *Bulletin of the BPS*, 33.

Popcorn, F. (1991) *The Popcorn Report*. New York: Harperbusiness.

Powney, J. and Watts, M. (1987) *Interviewing in Educational Research*. London: Routledge & Kegan Paul.

Robson, S. (1989) 'Validity and reliability in qualitative market research: the concept of fit', in *Proceedings of a MRDF (Market Research Society) Seminar on Reliability and Validity in Qualitative Research*. London: MRS. pp. 11–14.

Robson, S. and Wardle, J. (1988) 'Who's watching whom? A study of the effects of observers on group discussions', *Proceedings of the Market Research Society Conference*. London: MRS.

Rogers, C. and Roethlisberger, F.J. (1991) *Barriers and Gateways to Communication in Business Classics: Fifteen Key Concepts for Managerial Success*. Boston, MA: Harvard Business Review. pp. 12–18.

Rowan, J. (1983) *The Reality Game*. London: Routledge.

Sampson, P. (ed.) (1998) *Qualitative Research Through a Looking Glass*. Maidenhead: ESOMAR.

Schacter, D. (1996) *Searching for Memory: The Brain, the Mind and the Past*. New York: Basic Books.

Schutz, William (1958) *FIRO: A Three-Dimensional Theory of Interpersonal Behaviour*. New York: Holt, Rinehart, and Winston.

Seale, C. (1998) 'Qualitative interviewing', in C. Seale (ed.), *Researching Society and Culture*. London: Sage.

Sheth, Jagdish N. (1973) *Role of Motivation Research in Consumer Psychology*. Maidenhead: ESOMAR.

Spackman, N., Barker, A. and Nancarrow, C. (2000) 'Happy New Millennium: a research paradigm for the 21st century', *Proceedings of the Market Research Society Conference*. London: MRS. pp. 91–104.

Swindells, A. (2000) 'The invisible mechanism of consumption', *Proceedings of the Market Research Society Conference*. London: MRS. pp. 45–53.

Sykes, W. and Brandon, K. (1990) 'Qualitative research models: towards a typology', *Proceedings of the Market Research Society Conference*. London: MRS. pp. 165–76.

Tajfel, H. (1981) *Human Groups and Social Categories: Studies in Social Psychology*. Cambridge: Cambridge University Press.

Trevaskis, H. (2000) '"You had to be there". Why marketers are increasingly experiencing consumers for themselves and the impact of this on the role and remit of consumer professionals', *International Journal of Market Research*, 42 (1): 271–8.

Trinker, D. (1998) 'The Zombie within', *New Scientist*, 5 September.

Tuckman, B. (1965) 'Developmental sequence in small groups', *Psychological Bulletin*, 63: 384–99.

Valentine, V. (1996) 'Opening up the black box: switching the paradigm of qualitative research', *Marketing and Research Today*. May.

Valentine, V. and Evans, M. (1993) 'The dark side of the onion: rethinking the meanings of "rational" and "emotional" responses', *Journal of the Market Research Society*, 35 (2): 125–44.

Valentine, V. and Gordon, W. (2000) 'The 21st century consumer – a new model of thinking', *Proceedings of the Market Research Society Conference*. London: MRS. pp. 77–91.

Wardle, J. (2002) *Developing Advertising with Qualitative Market Research*. Book 6 in Gill Ereaut, Mike Imms and Martin Callingham (eds), *Qualitative Market Research* (7 volumes). London: Sage.

Yelland, F. and Varty, C. (1997) 'DIY: consumer-driven research', *Proceedings of the Market Research Society Conference*. London: MRS. pp. 89–100.

# Index